What People Are  Dan Willis and *Freedom to Forget*

Each of us has been hurt in the past. I began reading *Freedom to Forget* and couldn't put it down until I finished it. Pastor Dan made me face some still active wounds within me. He made me realize how, without me previously knowing it, those hurts had claimed control over portions of my life. Lovingly, Pastor Dan walked me through how to deal with the pain using godly principles and examples, helping me to look to the future instead of constantly staring at the rearview mirror.

—*Marvin Rhodes,*
Vice President of Operations,
TCT Network

Dan gets past the clichés and platitudes and down to where most of us live in *Freedom to Forget.* He gets so close to where I have lived that it's almost painful. But he has been there too, and he has the courage to admit it. The power of the book is not just in having insights into where we live, but a biblical way through the struggles and temptations we all face. This is an important book for Christians and non-Christians alike and it is definitely on my recommended reading list.

—*Dr. Jerry Rose,*
President/CEO,
Total Living Network

Freedom to Forget is the evidence that something good has happened in the life of a person desperate enough to accept God's loving effort to free them from themselves. Because we tend to live within ourselves, we can tend to forget all that God has in store for us. Our freedom comes when God helps us cut the cord to our baggage of past hurts, bruises, failures, and disappointments. Dan speaks to the brand-new life that we have when we grasp our "freedom" to move into the light of God's promises.

—*Pastor Ed Smith,*
Pastor of Trinity Christian Center, TBN

My friend, Rev. Dan Willis, a powerfully and passionately anointed messenger soldier and servant of the Lord Jesus Christ, shares his heart with us in *Freedom to Forget.* This work will be an empowering sensation to us all. Thank you for sharing yet another magnificent gift!

—*Sylvia St. James,*
National Talent Coordinator/Director,
House of Blues Sunday Gospel Brunch

FREEDOM TO FORGET

RELEASING THE PAIN FROM THE PAST, EMBRACING HOPE FOR THE FUTURE

DAN WILLIS

WHITAKER HOUSE

FREEDOM TO FORGET:
Releasing Pain from the Past, Embracing Hope for the Future

For speaking engagements, you may contact the author at:

The Lighthouse Church of All Nations 4501 W. 127th Street
Chicago's "Bridging the Gap" Church Alsip, IL 60803
(708) 385-6020 www.thelighthousechurch.org

ISBN: 978-0-88368-222-7
Printed in the United States of America
© 2007 by Dan Willis

1030 Hunt Valley Circle
New Kensington, PA 15068
www.whitakerhouse.com

Library of Congress Cataloging-in-Publication Data
Willis, Dan.
Freedom to forget : releasing pain from the past, embracing hope for the future / Dan Willis.
p. cm.
Summary: "Shows how dwelling on pain from the past can destroy a life, but forgetting past hurts and moving on is possible"—Provided by publisher.
ISBN 978-0-88368-222-7 (trade pbk. : alk. paper) 1. Forgiveness—Religious aspects—Christianity. 2. Attitude change—Religious aspects—Christianity. 3. Memory—Religious aspects—Christianity. 4. Pain—Religious aspects—Christianity. 5. Suffering—Religious aspects—Christianity. I. Title.
BV4647.F55W55 2007
248.8'6—dc22   2007011557

1 2 3 4 5 6 7 8 9 10 11 12 ⨀ 15 14 13 12 11 10 09 08 07

Credits

- Father God—whom I strive daily to make the Head of my life

- Linda, my life—for supporting me as I fulfill the passion that burns within me

- Melody, Rachel, Holly, and Chad—for making my life worth living

- Christopher—my silk-haired grandson, who loves peanuts in "Papa D's" office

- Ed and Lill Page—for providing me the sanctuary of their home in upper Michigan to complete this book

- Renee—for all the typing and retyping and retyping and...

- Debbie—above and beyond the call. I thank you so much

- VG and Ken, my editors—I only hope to "have a way with words" like you two someday

- Lighthouse Church—for allowing me to continue my "learning" with you for twenty years

- Mona and Terry—you are beautiful examples of Christian character, and I love you

- David Carney, general manager of All Nations Choir (formerly Pentecostals of Chicago) for loving to push and prod people to excel more than anyone I know

- T.L. & Nicki—for sparking my interest to even begin the first page

- Rod—the miracle of friendship against all odds

- Darius—you are "energy personified"

- J.R.—for always setting the example of "It'll all work out"

- Tito—a man after God's own heart... Jonathan to a David

- Finally, I humbly dedicate this writing to you, dear reader—in honor of your attempt to go forward! *May God's Very Best Be Yours!*

Contents

Prologue

Prologue

I have purchased many "how to" books in my twenty-eight years as a pastor. *How to Serve. How to Love. How to Improve Your Memory.* Even with that last title, I have forgotten much of what I may have read, and where I put the books when I finished! I haven't a clue where most of them are today.

However, while encouraging people in self-help skills and ways to improve themselves when dealing with contemporary issues and problems, I discovered something quite amazing: *Most of us do not need as much help **remembering** as we do **forgetting**!* We are locked in a swirling cesspool that holds us hostage to the past and thwarts future progress by reminding us of all that has transpired and brought pain into our life. It may be things such as

- secret sexual sin
- the loss of a loved one
- unforgiveness

Whatever the problem, I pray that within the pages of this book, you will find help and strength to go forward as you find the *Freedom to Forget*.

—*Rev. Dan Willis*
Alsip, Illinois

Chapter 1

The First Step

Chapter 1

The First Step

"Ashes to ashes, dust to dust..."

Snow...

ice...

freezing cold...

and a tiny white casket
resting softly on a white
winter blanket over Chicago...

This is how I would remember the day, when, as a young preacher, I had to stand before that grieving young couple. She was weak from the birth, weeping and huddled against her husband. He was stoic, hardened, not wanting to show that he was, understandably, hurting.

This was neither their first attempt to have a baby, nor the second, nor even the third, but the fourth. *A baby.* We had all hoped so strongly this pregnancy would be the one. She would make it. We even shared "church" in their living room in the months before she would give birth. This time they were taking no chances. The fourth month passed—praise God. The fifth month came, farther than ever. The sixth month passed, which meant the baby could now live on its own outside the womb if she delivered early. Even the beginning of a seventh month of pregnancy came. Then, it was over. No amount of tears, trying to see from a bigger perspective, or spiritual guidance would erase the grief.

Now, here we were at the gravesite. I remember weeping as I drove up that winter day, stepping out, seeing that hardened father, and wanting to question God myself, wanting to run. I couldn't run away, though. I was their pastor. I was needed. It was my job to console them and give them the answers to the questions they had. Why

Eventually, our unresolved hurts will surface— most likely as bitterness, hardness, and anger at others or even at God.

had this happened? Where was God? Words seemed to evade me, and though more than twenty-five years have since passed, my memory is still etched with what happened that day. I closed my Bible, folded my notes into my little black *Star Book for Ministers*, said a short prayer, held their hands, and just cried with them. They didn't need a spoken sermon at that moment; instead they needed a quiet reminder of God's comforting presence and love—and quite honestly, so did I.

 Freedom to Forget

Later I would reprimand myself for being such an amateur. Surely, an experienced preacher would know just what to say. Now, all these years later, I realize God was just teaching me how to "sing the hard songs." Sometimes the answers are not enough and you feel you cannot go on. You want to run away and forget, but every detail leaps more vividly from the anguished recesses of your wounded soul the farther you run. That is the time to cry. Just cry.

We cried together, not in self-pity or martyrdom, but a heart-wrenching cry to our Father God for strength to "please, just get us through this horrible moment in time." We survived. We went to work. We ate again, read the newspaper, took a walk, and cried some more when the grief was overwhelming. Then one day, we smiled, and eventually a laugh came.

From this tragic moment, early in my ministry, I learned that the first step to forgetting the vicious blows that life and others often deal us is realizing that we do not always need to understand—to wrap our brain around the immensity of those traumatic moments. Sometimes, we just need to honestly hurt in the moment. We can find comfort in the companionship of our Lord and quietly hold on to a few close friends or family members who understand we do not need words of consolation or a sermon but rather someone who will just weep with us while we are hurting.

A sure way to engrave a tragic moment into your memory, making it much harder to later put behind you, is not to hurt in the moment and do the appropriate grieving. If we forcefully stuff our unresolved hurts into the dark alcoves of our minds, they will fester in our psyches like a splinter that gets infected. Eventually, they will surface: most likely as bitterness, hardness, and anger at others or even God.

Today, that grieving mother remains faithful, does numerous clerical jobs for the church, and even organizes special events. Her husband is a pastor's friend, someone who found his way back to a loving God, just trusting His infinite wisdom. He supports the ministry of our church in every way and would probably give up everything to see us survive!

> Comfort can be found in the companionship of our Lord and through friends and family members.

There are pains in this world that we cannot explain in our human understanding. But as this story illustrates, healing is possible. What do you do when your mind cannot be still and the hurt is making it impossible to move on with life? It is very common for us to rehash our hurts rather than letting them go. Instead of letting our wounds heal, we keep picking away at the scabs of memory, making ourselves bleed anew. This is the time we must practice forgetfulness. In the next chapters, I am going to discuss specific steps you can take to forget the pain of the past. It is possible to remember the events of your past without

unleashing the debilitating emotions associated with them. Then you are free to move on toward the future.

The first step is to cry, shout, let it out—until He tells you, "Let it go." Cry until the revelation of "Your will is what's best for me"[1] assuages the grief. Lean not on your own understanding (Proverbs 3:5), but rather lean upon God's comforting presence as you lament and purge your heart of the pain. You will go on; you will learn to forget the pain!

---

[1] "Your Will," words and music by Darius Brooks from *Your Will* by Darius Brooks, © 2004, EMI Gospel.

Chapter 2

Lose the Details

Chapter 2

Lose the Details

W"*here did you put my striped shirt?*" I had asked everyone in the house, including my three-year-old son; the only one left to ask was the dog. And then there it was—hanging right where my wife said it would be, where *I* had hung it (and then blamed everyone else for losing it). It was my fault, but I could not remember.

Why is my short-term memory faulty, while I can remember pain and hurts from long ago with excruciating detail? Why can't we forget those things just as easily? I will tell you why: because we treat them differently! We methodically store them up and enhance the "tracking" controls; we dust off the drama of it all, until it becomes our complete focus! We can let little things go, sometimes very important little things, like our anniversary or where we put our keys; whereas those painful memories are *self-proclaimed landmarks* that we don't let go of.

If you are ever going to survive your emotional disasters, the next thing you have to do is *stop rehearsing the details!* "Was it four o'clock? Or three-thirty? Maybe it was just after noon." Who cares what time your husband walked out? The fact is *he is gone.* Those little details (*"little foxes"* the Bible calls them) will destroy your sanity (*"spoil the vine"*). (See Song of Solomon 2:15.) They are draining your physical strength, biting deep into your emotional well-being, and inspiring every negative thought imaginable. With each recollection of the specifics, the event becomes more permanently imprinted in your memory. The devil doesn't need to keep reminding you of your past—you are destructive enough on your own! Stop the summer reruns, the endless encore performances. Pick up your chips and dip and turn that mental video off.

The devil doesn't need to keep reminding you of your past—you are destructive enough on your own!

When it starts, wherever you are, change your mind flow. One of the best ways I have found to do this is to get with a crowd. Staying home alone only contributes to feelings of isolation, loneliness, and depression. Drive to the mall, go grocery shopping, and if it is a church night, certainly that is where you must go. Allow no excuses for yourself. Get with other human beings. But when you are with others, do not talk about yourself and your problems. Listen to their troubles for a while.

 Freedom to Forget

You may say, "How can I help someone else when I cannot even help myself?" As you listen, you (and the Lord, in you) will be touched by the feelings of their fractured hearts, and you will then give advice or comfort. A strange phenomena will then occur: while listening to yourself, you will hear your mouth speak the right things to do. Your soul will articulate, and you will know what you should start doing: listen to your own advice!

Slowly, you will find that, as you stop rehearsing the details, they will lose their potency. If for some reason you must recall the events—maybe for the purpose of ministry, in order to demonstrate an empathetic understanding of what someone else is going through—then recount it in more general terms. It happened, and you can't change it, but you can acknowledge the facts without giving it power over your emotions. Eventually the generalities will become the highlights in place of the specifics. Do this and you will start to forget.

If the feelings return, the first thing you should do is pray: "Dear God, I cannot do this without You. Please take it, take it *all*—and please take it now." You will reach the place where you have given it to God, your mind is emptied, your emotions spent, and you can sleep peacefully. Be assured, the sun will shine in the morning!

Chapter 3

Understanding Is Not Necessary

Chapter 3

Understanding Is Not Necessary

A few years ago I woke up and was all set to feel despondent, blue, and quiet, because it was November 6—my thirty-eighth birthday. As I pulled my "I'm-going-on-a-diet-after-today" body into the motions of "ho-humness"—anticipating that the highlight of the day would be filling out an application for McDonald's 25-cent senior citizens' cup of coffee program—I suddenly realized that, for the first time in my life, my waist size was smaller than my age! Then I went from threatening my children not to mention that it even was my birthday to telling anyone who would listen about my most amazing day when I got even with life. I was all set to complain but then started smiling (albeit with a few more lines carved into my face around that smile) and feeling pretty good anyhow.

Sometimes we cannot understand ourselves, and yet we spend so much time trying to understand life.

If some of the definitions of *spend* are "use up, wear out, waste, squander," then that means we *waste* a lot of time worrying about things we cannot change. We use up irretrievable minutes and hours of our precious allotment of time on this earth trying to figure things out, only to have them change again as soon as we have made progress. We are spending our inheritance (time) unwisely. You cannot understand all things, all the time, about all people or all situations. Sometimes you must just accept life as it is unfolding in front of you.

We consume a tremendous amount of time worrying over our relationships in this way. "Why did he say that?" "What did she mean by that?" "I just can't understand what possessed him to act that way!" Marriage, children, and best friendships *spend* us. I have almost blown more than one relationship because either I could not understand

Thank God for the diversity around us. He didn't create life to make it boring.

them or they could not understand me. Then one day, when faced with the choice of losing a dear friend, I came to grips with the bottom line—relationships are often not about *understanding* one another as much as they are about just *accepting* one another.

If everyone really did everything the way I thought they should do it, what a bunch of clones would fill my life, and how boring that would be! Let me just get ugly here for a second: to all those who act like they have been sprayed with holiness and blow-dried with sanctification—if everybody were like you, who would you talk about? If no one had big hair or some serious bell-bottoms or passé styles to call the fashion police on, some of us would not have anything to look at while window-shopping in the mall. I'm not saying that we should mock those who are different, but we should thank God for the diversity around us. He didn't create life in order to make it boring.

So often the energy we spend on trying to *understand* others is Satan's ploy to keep us from *accepting* and *loving* those whom God places around us.

- The mother who cannot understand why her son is gay learns to love him anyway—not to love his lifestyle, but to love *him*.

- The friend who cannot understand why punctuality is unimportant to his best friend learns to plan things with an extra half hour built in rather than just abandon the relationship.

- The young lady abused by her father as a child decides once and for all, "I will never be able to go back to being a little girl again and redo my childhood. I don't know why my dad hurt me, but I forgive him through God's help, and I will not allow what happened to keep me from who I was created to be. I cannot live in the past, so I will just raise my hands up to a *heavenly* Father and say, 'I have languished long enough trying to figure it out.' From this moment on I will boldly declare, 'It matters not so much where I have been as it does where I'm going.'"

Forgetting those things which are behind, and reaching forth unto those things which are before. (Philippians 3:13)

Don't expend time and effort trying to understand the incomprehensible. Make up your mind today, "If I *never* understand, I will just keep walking with You, Jesus. When I get to glory, if it is still important, You can tell me all about why I had to go through that situation or lose that loved one, *but I have to get there first!*"

> If you never understand why things have happened in your life, just keep walking with Jesus.

When I began pastoring at age sixteen, there were few people who believed the church would make it. We had lost our pastor as a small congregation in its infancy. The first Sunday I pastored, we had only sixteen people. Since I was evidently the one with the "gift of talking" (as one dear sister put it), I was just going to "hold things together" until we could get a new pastor. Well, we found out quickly there were not many ministers beating the door down to pastor sixteen people with no pay, no benefits, and no certainty of the future survival of our small congregation. So, I prayed, then preached and "talked" my way through until we finally realized that this was God's perfect plan for my life. I had been called to build a "bridging the gap" church (one that focused on inclusivity in regards to race, culture, and background) in the city of Chicago for all people.

We made it through those first few difficult years due to the few precious people who did not try to understand but simply accepted the situation and believed we could still build a church for the cause of Christ despite the circumstances. One was a single mother who worked many long hours to support her family; she loved the work of God so deeply and was determined to see a church in Chicago. I can still remember her selfless sacrifices, like the time she knew we had an electric bill due and no money to pay it. She came to my office and signed over her entire paycheck, adamant that the "work of the Lord must go on." I am sure you can see why this dear soul meant so much to a young pastor. She truly was a rare jewel.

I will never forget the night she told me she had been diagnosed with terminal breast cancer. I cried and cried, and truly believed that if God would heal anyone, He would definitely heal her. My heart broke as I looked at her fifty-five-pound body the night she drew her last breaths, because I could not understand why she would have to suffer and die and not somebody else—perhaps someone who did not care as much about Lighthouse Church and me.

Then, in a way that I will never forget, the Lord's words came to me, "Child, if you never understand why, you just keep walking with Me. When you get *here*, I'm going to make it all plain for you, but you have to get here first, Dan." From that day on, I determined I would never be bitter at God and grab for excuses that lead to irresponsibility and failure just because I did not understand. I would instead cling to Him and accept that He can bring me through anything. When I get to heaven, He will tell me. And He will surely tell you too.

From that incident came this song:

If my hands are never held
And if my love is never felt
And if this cup never passes from me,
Then I'll understand just what Jesus did for me.

If your name they only abuse
And if your words they only misuse
And if your heart someone's broken in two
Then you'll understand just what Jesus did for you

Understand, yes, I'll understand
The road to Calvary and no one to hold His hand

So if the burdens you carry
Make it hard to keep up the pace,
You've got to remember it will be worth it
When we see His face.

And when we see our King Jesus
And know that we've won this race
We'll understand it better.
It's true there's no tears in heaven.

Crying, "Holy, holy is the Lamb,"
At last before His throne I'll stand.
Then He'll understand and say, "Well done."

"Understand" words and music Rev. Dan Willis from *Stand* by
Rev. Dan Willis & the Pentecostals of Chicago, ©1995, Tyscot, Inc.

Chapter 4

Over the Rough Terrain

Chapter 4

Over the Rough Terrain

Y ou are going to go from point A to point B, but the ride is up to you.

God has a plan for your life, and—even if you feel like you are stationary—something, somewhere, right now is being moved on your behalf. Often we think we will never get past today's problem, but then next week or next year, you suddenly find yourself at "point B." God is in control of your departure and arrival times; the only thing you control is the quality (your attitude) of the ride.

Traveling from Chicago to St. Louis takes six hours by car. If you take a car with tires that are threadbare, have bubbles, and need air, your ride is going to be bumpy and precarious—not to mention stressful, given the uncertainty of actually arriving at your destination. On the other hand, if your car has new all-season radial tires that are balanced and properly inflated, your ride is going to be much smoother. Both cars may get you from point A to point B, but the difference is in the ride!

It is inevitable: you are going to have suffering in this life. You will cry. You will be misunderstood, and you will often not understand, but point B is still coming! You can choose to travel the road in a "buggy of bolts" (as my mother used to say), an attitude filled with stress and anxiety—all of which still will not make your husband come back, the fever go away, or money appear in your account; or you can choose to square your shoulders, lift your head up, and enjoy the ride. As the apostle Paul said, *"I have learned, in whatsoever state I am, therewith to be content"* (Philippians 4:11).

God's plan for your life incorporates all the twists and turns and still designs to bless you and keep you.

There are people who have wasted years of their lives being negative and stressed out about getting to point B. They still arrived at point B, for no situation lasts forever, but God allows us to choose—relaxed and trusting or hanging on for dear life, yelling at the driver.

Know that God is able to see points A, B, and even C through Z, and has a multitude of positive thoughts toward you and definite plans to bring you there! It is not like God just woke up today and suddenly got a clue about what is going on in your life and then had to concoct a whole new strategy for bringing success in your life. His plan incorporates all the twists and turns—and yes, even the tragedies—and *still* has you coming up to point B with designs to bless you and keep you for point C and beyond. Listen to the heart of God in one of my favorite passages,

> *"For I know the plans I have for you," declares the LORD, "plans to prosper you and not to harm you, plans to give you hope and a future."*
> (Jeremiah 29:11 NIV)

A big part of learning to forget has to do with trusting God, knowing that He will use the bruised knees and sore tailbones to get you to point B and beyond. God can use what others have meant for harm to bring about good in our lives. (See Genesis 50:20.) When we recognize this, we will be more apt to let go of some of the smoldering coals of unforgiveness and even start moving toward putting the pain of harmful episodes in our lives behind us.

Several years ago, while preparing to record a live album in Jamaica, I became stressed and obsessed with the fact that the producer could not be at the first rehearsal. Then, only two days after he informed me of this "disaster," my phone rang with an offer for the choir to be a part of a major television production on the very date of that first rehearsal. So you see? God had to rearrange our producer's schedule (point A) because He already knew we were going to need that date free (point B), so we could accommodate this very important event (point C) and be blessed according to God's design. God saw the whole process at one glance, while I saw only one point. When it was all said and done, I realized *I* had determined the conditions of my ride to point B and C and probably added a few wrinkles and gray hairs with self-induced stress that was *totally* unnecessary.

So, just relax, sing, smile, and do your best to enjoy life, knowing in your heart that God's plan is still in effect, that He will meet you at the end of the day, and that He surely will not be worried about the outcome.

Chapter 4

Does True Forgiving Mean Instant Forgetting?

Chapter 5

Does True Forgiving Mean Instant Forgetting?

Case before the court: "Have you really forgiven?"
Prosecution's exhibit A:
"You can still remember what happened."
"Objection, your honor!"

So many people feel like frauds because they have heard someone (maybe even a preacher) say, "If you have truly forgiven, you will have forgotten." They feel guilty and as if they are second-class Christians because they have not forgotten. Relax. Forgiveness is an *act of the will*. Because it is an act of the will, expunging the memory is not a prerequisite; neither is it an instant result.

However, make no mistake. Forgiveness often needs help from you because, even though it is an act of the will, the emotional scars will bring back to remembrance the injury and try to convince you to resurrect unforgiveness. For instance, you see that person who hurt you emotionally, and you feel flushed and sweaty as the original anger and hurt returns. At that moment you must "coach" yourself through it—talk to yourself right then. Reaffirm, "I settled that, and I refuse to waste even five seconds more on this subject." (Just because a kid hits a home run today does not mean he has forgotten how to strike out. That is why he must be continually coached.)

I am not telling you to avoid working through your problems with that person. You can't ignore your emotions, pretend to be happy, and expect the hurt to go away. You must choose to forgive the person. Then, when the bad feelings resurface, you can choose not to give place to them. Don't let bitterness take one more second of your life.

Don't let bitterness rob you of joy for one second more in your life. Coach yourself to be positive.

How do you know five seconds of negativity now will not mean five seconds off the end of your life? Even if it doesn't actually shorten your life, it is five seconds wasted that could have been put to better use. I don't know about you, but I do not want to lose even five seconds! With some, those five seconds have added up to months and years. The problem is, we spend time re-covering ground that has already been covered. The fact that you experience residual emotions does not prove you did not forgive. It just means you need to remind your emotions to work with your will. Save your energy! Work with your coach!

Often we do not realize that there is such a big disconnect between the seat of our emotions (our hearts) and the framework of our rational, logical selves (our minds). I have discovered that we can be bitter in our hearts and mentally be in denial about our lack of forgiveness. Once we accept that we truly are still holding onto a grudge in our hearts, it is important that we coach ourselves again and again with the truths that will set us free of that attitude and will, in turn, soften our hearts and persuade our emotional selves to "let go" of the need to hold on, self-protect, and execute punishment on those who have hurt us.

> If God has forgiven you, the forgiveness you have to give is also God's. Don't withhold it.

Eventually, your diligent efforts (coaching) will provide a "reverse Novocain" to the pain; the discomfort is eliminated at the end of the procedure, not the beginning. Your heart will eventually get weary of reiterating the emotional list of grievances to a brain that is only going to say, "Save your energy." But if you do not take the initiative to start talking to your heart today, you will waste precious opportunities to enjoy life. God will not be the one leaving these destructive "Post-It® notes" on the desktop of your memory—Satan is the *"accuser of the brethren"* (Revelation 12:10) and loves to remind us of our past hurts and other's failures (it's kind of a hobby of his). However, the Word of God "coaches" me that when Satan reminds me of the past, I am to remind him of his future. Better yet, I need to keep reminding myself of the glorious future God has in store for me.

So, if God has forgiven you, you have an obligation to give forgiveness in return. Your "pitcher of forgiveness" was filled by Him, and it is not yours to withhold from anyone. First of all, there are free refills, and second, the only way you can get a refill for yourself is to give God's forgiveness away to others.

Following that, you need to tell somebody that you have forgiven. People always chuckle when I quite often stop to say, "You better tell somebody" in the middle of my sermons. In this case, the power and need for accountability kicks in. When you tell someone you have forgiven the person who hurt you, and then later the pain surfaces again—which it will do as it is working out of your system—you will be reminded that you went out on a limb and made a decision to forgive. You even confessed that to others, and no one wants to make a liar out of themselves. When you confess to God, your intimate confidants, and maybe even nearby acquaintances that you have forgiven a person, you have taken a major step toward releasing and thereby forgetting the sting of the offense. We overcome by the blood of the Lamb (God's provision to do the forgiveness) and by the word of our testimony (our ownership of our God-aided response to the offense).

What is the cost of not doing this? Well, the spiritual and emotional ramifications are dire, not to mention the *cosmetic* effects of unforgiveness. Look at people who harbor unforgiveness. They are often stoic, with a permanent frown carved into what used to be a pretty face. They think children laughing in the backseat are rude, and it has been way too long since they laughed so hard they cried. There is no doubt forgiveness gives you the same feeling as stepping on the scale and realizing you lost weight! A weight of a different kind has dropped off your heart and mind, making you feel light and free. It's time to celebrate!

So, let's drop all those unsightly pounds of *unforgiveness*, and step up on the scale. Coaching yourself will help you stay young. I dare you to try talking to yourself.

A wise friend of mine reminds me continually, "Forgive first—the feeling will come later." Then, to lock it in, you better tell somebody!

Chapter 6

Smiling in the Funeral Parlor

Chapter 6

Smiling in the Funeral Parlor

At age seventeen, as a new husband, I was also going to college full-time, working full-time, and trying to build a congregation full-time. Money was occasionally a problem—at least six or seven days a week! In order to support my new bride and everything else I was involved in, I became staff chaplain at a local funeral home. For every funeral I preached, I made money—fifty dollars a pop usually. We were so "mournfully" elated at those last-minute calls from the funeral home. I never knew the people, and I promise you I did my best. I cried many times at funerals of people I had never met (not hypocritically—I was sincerely moved by the grief of their loved ones).

The local undertaker and I worked together often. He taught me that to survive in that business, you *had* to keep a sense of humor, albeit a warped one. I could not look at him as he stood in the back of the funeral parlor while I performed my liturgical duties or he would crack me up. He definitely learned that *joy* was the "forgetting" medicine.

I began to realize, through seeing so much grief and mourning on a regular basis, that it was no wonder why Satan tried to steal our joy.

I have heard preaching on this subject all my life and have even routinely repeated it myself. The theme is this: the devil wants our holiness, morals, youth, marriages, and traditions. While I have no doubt all of that is true, I have observed something different. I believe the devil goes straight for the jugular vein of any church—their *joy*.

If the devil steals your joy, he automatically has a hold on everything else.

If he can get our joy, he has an automatic hold on everything else! A person who loses his or her joy no longer cares about holiness, morals, marriage, going to work, singing in the choir, or anything else. So, the enemy does not waste time going after those things. Stealing your joy is a "one-stop shopping spree" for him. Why waste time chopping off the individual branches when you can do the job so much more swiftly, and with such devastation, by going for the trunk of the tree?

Think about it: when your joy is gone, you get depressed and don't care about anything else. For that reason, the best way to forget after you forgive is to start laughing again—and soon! It is a great medicine for the process of healing. Take the funeral clothes off. Quit preparing to be unhappy. Buy a "just for fun" card that will make someone howl with laughter. Listen to polka music and sing with it—whether you can sing or not. Sing and dance. Look for the funny things that happen at church. Christians often have more fun accidentally than the world has on purpose, and afterward there are no regrets or hangovers.

Every time I need a lift to make it through, I remember a humorous little story that happened to a minister friend of mine at a funeral.

He was an older gentleman and had arrived at the funeral home a few minutes late, which will already set you on edge if you are the clergy in charge, which he was. He was met at the door by the widow, who was not a churchgoer. Since the deceased was, however, she wanted to fulfill her husband's wishes.

Her husband had requested music.

There was no one to sing.

So, she hastened to the kind preacher as he arrived. "Sir, would you please do me a huge favor? I need you to sing a song before you give the eulogy for my husband."

"Oh, no. Oh, no, no, no! I am not a singer."

"Oh, please!"

"No. No. I just couldn't."

"Oh, sir, please! You *must! My* husband wanted his favorite song sung. Please, pastor, please!"

Then he considered the fact that he had arrived late, and she was being so very insistent about this. Finally, with *extreme* reluctance, he said, "Alright, what song?"

She considered carefully for a moment, trying to remember his favorite song, and then requested, "Please sing his favorite song, 'Jingle Bells.'"

Well, you can imagine his reaction. But her pleas persisted until he relented again and walked somberly to the front of the tiny, darkly lit chapel. He stopped in front of the little podium to the right of the casket, and—to the small gathering of bereaved—he began to sing. He struggled mightily to sing the best mournful, funereal, dirge-like, minor-keyed way he could muster, slowly rendering a heartbroken chorus of "Jingle bells, jingle bells, jingle all the way. Oh, what fun it is to ride...."

How he got through it, I could never imagine, people crying and wailing at "in a one-horse open sleigh."

He finished singing. He spoke. He prayed. He ended the service.

As the wife came around for the final "thank you" to the old minister, she touched his hand and said, "Thank you so much, Reverend. I am so sorry, though. I gave you the wrong song. It was supposed to be 'When They Ring Those Golden Bells.'"

Now, if that does not make you smile or chuckle a bit, then maybe your sense of humor needs new life

breathed into it. I know it can be uncouth to smile in a funeral parlor, but isn't it better to remember things with a smile than with a frown? And may I add that the Christian man was rejoicing with his Savior in heaven? He certainly had no need for tears! The Scriptures tell us, *"A merry heart does good like a medicine"* (Proverbs 17:22). A big part of the healing process and learning to forget is remembering to smile and laugh again.

Chapter 7

Keep Hope Alive

Chapter 7

Keep Hope Alive

Question: What is an eternal optimist?
Answer: One who refuses to let hope
take a rest.

There is no feeling comparable to that instantaneous burst of "it will be okay" that comes eventually. You suddenly feel like eating again, or taking a walk, or going out on a date. It comes when the clouds part, just for a moment, to let you see that the sun is shining again. Then you know you *will* survive and everything is going to be all right.

I remember the first time I heard Reverend Jesse Jackson say, "Keep hope alive!" I began to realize that if people in this city did not have a car, they could still go on. If they did not have fancy clothes, they could still make it. Even if they did not have a family, they could survive. But if the catalyst of hope dissipated, they could not go on.

Proverbs tells us that, *"Hope deferred makes the heart sick, but a longing fulfilled is a tree of life"* (Proverbs 13:12).

Over the years I have been involved in Chuck Colson's Prison Fellowship Ministry. I have ministered to countless numbers of young men and women in prisons all across this country. You will never meet people whose hearts are more despondent than the incarcerated. They do not have a lot of hope about the future.

I remember one young Christian man telling me the story of his first night and having that large steel door slammed shut behind him. He described a feeling of being overwhelmed, almost to the point of not being able to breathe. He told me that he just sat there the entire first night, in the dark, staring at the wall, wondering how his life had come to that point.

When the sun came up in the morning, just a single dime-sized ray of light was able to make it into his cell. The moment it was able to penetrate into where he was, it hit the very spot he had been staring at all night long. Inscribed on the wall, unseen throughout the night, were the words, "I will have better days."

He instantly knew those words, hidden in the dark—until the *light* shined upon them—were a message directly from heaven. God knew where he was and was going to use even this to bring about His purposes in his life. From that day on, the man had a contentment that passed understanding (see

Philippians 4:7) about where he was and how God was going to use his time in prison to turn his life around. He is now out, living for God, and one of the best Bible teachers I have ever heard.

There have been more than a few Sundays over the last twenty years of pastoring when I ended the day of services and activities feeling like a dismal failure. Perhaps finances were low, attendance was bad (or at least not what I thought it should be), the music was a disaster (at least by the standard of what I knew it could be), kids cried, people walked out, I felt like my message was not as articulate as I had planned, and no one came to the altar for salvation. (Hopefully, not all of this occured on the same Sunday, but sometimes it felt like it.) In those moments we are most vulnerable.

At the moments when you are most vulnerable, remember what the Lord has done in the past to bring you through.

Satan does not play fair. He does not try to make you feel like giving up when you are feeling major "swoops" of victory. He is cunning. He waits until you are down on yourself and low on hope that things will ever get better. Then, he is only too happy to validate those feelings.

In moments of temporary despondency, I have seen good men leave their wives and/or the churches they pastored, leaving a wake of destruction behind them.

I have sometimes felt like giving up myself, but I developed a self-help cure to forget those miserable times.

When you feel like you have not accomplished what you hoped, do not give up. Do not base your decision on a one-day evaluation. You must look back over the entire span, not just one day. For me, that translates to this: "Okay, today was not the best, but, Dan, you started out with sixteen people. Look at how far the Lord has brought you over the last twenty-eight years—a new miraculous piece of property, a multi-million dollar building project, 1,400 members, a solid marriage, and healthy children and grandchildren.

When mentoring developing ministers, I often encourage them, "When you look back at the disaster of the day, ask yourself at that moment, working with all the dynamics you had going on (physical, health, microphones, heat, cold, time restraints), did you do your best with what you had?" If they can answer yes, then I tell them, "Friend, God is pleased, because in our weakness He becomes strong—and continues to be even after the sermon ends!"

Look for the "praise reports"—they are there if you just look. Call them out verbally. On those Sundays when I thought of giving up, I learned to say, "There's always next Sunday." Sure enough, many souls would be saved the next week, finances would go back up, and the choir would rock.

When people do not show up for choir rehearsal, encourage the director to forget about this week's attendance and tell him, "We will have better days." When the pastor's wife feels like her well-planned Christmas program did not go very well at all, just remind her that there is always next Christmas, and now she has more experience!

Keep hope alive! And, as you help others keep hope alive, your hope will increase. Even if it seems daunting, trivial, crazy—whatever—just find somebody, something, somehow, some way to hang on to your hope.

One of the ways I have had success in this realm is by *"speaking to yourselves in psalms and hymns and spiritual songs, singing and making melody in your heart to the Lord"* (Ephesians 5:19). I do not actually think this is about talking to yourself, but rather repeating biblical truths that encourage you. We should not rely upon getting more encouragement from others that better days are ahead than from God's Word and our own selves. As long as a brighter day is on the horizon, we can keep on keeping on. There is a brighter day on the horizon of forgetting those things that are behind, so if you have asked for hope, you must walk in it, and it will sustain you, but you have to keep hope alive!

Chapter 8

The Preventative Medicine of
Consistent Gratitude

Chapter 8

The Preventative Medicine of Consistent Gratitude

I n the last few years, I have started delaying my entrance into the sanctuary until the service starts. I often shake hands with a few people as I cross the sanctuary, but I do not try to take too much time to allow anyone to say much to me. Some may believe that I am doing this as a result of the church getting larger or more impersonal. Nothing could be farther from the truth! It has nothing to do with congregation size or me being on some ego trip. It allows me to stay focused on the task at hand, and I have adopted this process from years of getting slammed with some emotional bomb just before trying to step to the platform to worship and minister.

I will never forget the time I was unquestionably feeling a very special anointing for the service and for the message God had given—a message I had been praying and studying about for some weeks. As I entered the sanctuary, a precious saint of God walked up to me and whispered that her husband was cheating on her with someone in the congregation (who was sitting there) and that she desperately needed to meet with me for some damage control and counseling as soon as she could. I do not have to tell you how difficult it was for me to focus on that service and on worshipping God, much less on the message I needed to deliver for the benefit of God's people—people who were hungry and had come to hear just such a message.

Besides the critical element of a daily prayer life, one of the true secrets I have discovered in living my life unto the Lord is to continually maintain an attitude of gratitude. I am positive the load would have easily broken me had I not pulled alongside the Spirit of Christ in gratitude for His shepherding me and cast my burdens upon Him through prayer. I am aware that when I say "attitude of gratitude," many of you may initially think I am just firing an empty cliché over the bow of your ship. We must develop and maintain a spiritual reflex that instinctively responds with gratefulness; it is a powerful weapon in the battle against acidic bitterness.

Praise God in true thanksgiving for all the wonderful blessings He has given you.

If I had not developed an attitude of impulsive thankfulness early in my ministry, I would have easily been sidetracked, sideswiped, or even knocked completely off the path I am diligently trying to travel. I have learned to be grateful and praise and worship God with a heart filled with thankfulness for the many wonderful blessings He has bestowed upon me and the provision in my life. But I have also learned to have an attitude of thankfulness in advance of what God is going to do with a negative situation I am facing, knowing that He works out all things for good, because I love Him and am called according to His purpose. (See Romans 8:28.)

I have discovered the need and the blessing to having a preprogrammed knee-jerk reaction in my spirit of being thankful to God. If I did not regularly remind myself to have this mind-set, it would not be nearly as consistent as I need. Whether the Lord takes or gives, I try to make my first reaction gratitude. I make every effort to do this before digesting the news, evaluating its consequences or considering the implications. I do this out of the knowledge that God is directing my life, and this attitude goes directly to the concept that there are no coincidences, mistakes, or accidents in my life, since He is, in fact, in control.

When I am faced with a blessing or trial and my first reaction is gratitude, I have found that my response is almost always the right one. No one likes bad news, me less than most. However, when it comes, I immediately look to God and give Him praise and show that I am grateful toward Him, knowing that even this will somehow work out to my benefit. Afterward, when my heart wants to leap up in my throat, and the palpitations come from a surge of fear as I really consider what I might be facing, it is easier to coach my emotions and say, "No, my immediate response was right. I am indeed thankful unto God, and I will look to the hills from where my help comes. (See Psalm 121:1.) I will stand assured that God has it all under control: this too shall pass."

An attitude of consistent gratitude like this brings us into the right frame of mind. It makes our emotional first response to submit even this to God, jumping on the solution instead of assigning blame. It enables us to daily overcome offenses, pain, and so on, leaving you less to forgive and then to forget. You want to learn how to forget? Make up your mind to be consistently grateful about what-

Develop the habit of jumping on the solution instead of assigning blame.

ever comes your way. Think of it as the Lipitor of your spiritual life flow: it keeps the channels clear of dangerous build-up and clogs, leading to less opportunity for "hardening of your spiritual arteries."

If you are not consistent, your emotions are apt to respond unchecked. You may come upon a tough day and turn off onto the route of bitterness, anger, and hatred before you even realize it and not recover for some time—leaving yourself with even more things to forgive and later to forget.

Chapter 9

Exhaustion Causes You to Remember

Chapter 9

Exhaustion Causes You to Remember

"Don't look to the bigness of your need, look to the bigness of your God. Our circumstances are often hindrances to seeing God's ability."
—Morris Cerullo

It is amazing how the sound of my five-year-old strumming his toy guitar and singing loudly on Sunday night, after I have preached three services, sounds so differently than on Monday afternoon, when I am rested. The very thing I crave the next day is the thing I cringed at the night before. The circumstance did not change; I did, the result of putting myself to bed and recovering my serotonin levels. No wonder God's Word says, *"He gives his beloved sleep"* (Psalm 127:2 NKJV).

Have you ever felt a "wrenching" in the pit of your stomach? It is the feeling of being beyond overwhelmed.

Things are never as time consuming as kids needing a ride to different places, all at once, on your only day to sleep in. (Of course, they have no problems getting up early on Saturdays.) Things usually cost twice as much and take three times as long as you originally planned. You have more Christmas presents to buy and wrap than you have money or time for. There are too many "ugly" situations pulling for your attention, in a limited period of time, leading you to feeling overwhelmed.

When we become overwhelmed, other past negative situations (even those you have resolved) have a way of jumping back on the bus and riding into your life again. The key to times like those is remembering things are never as hard as you anticipate they will be when you are feeling overwhelmed or just plain tired.

You will always be better equipped to handle the trials that come your way if you are well rested.

I cannot tell you how many times in counseling people, I have told them they just need to go home, go to bed, and get some sleep. Not because I was trying to remove them from my office, but because *for overwhelmed people, often the only thing between them and complete despair is a good night's rest.* Rule number one: when you are rested, you can better handle anything God allows to come your way. Rule number

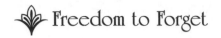

two: do not burn yourself out trying to override rule number one!

The first thing that is going to try and jump on the overwhelmed bus and crowd out current priorities will be the "old stuff" that you have had a hard time forgetting and letting go of. You will find yourself crying over things that have nothing to do with what overwhelmed you in the first place. For example, you are running late and cannot find a parking space, the kids are screaming, no one has eaten, your license is at home, your coat is stuck in the door and your contact lens is drying up, when you suddenly start crying due to the fact that no one loves you or needs you because when other kids went to the prom, no one asked you. All this out of nowhere! All of a sudden, you are *overwhelmed!*

For this reason, we must ever guard against complete exhaustion creeping up on us, or we are only asking for trouble in forgetting past pain. I know it may sound simple, but taking time off and sometimes just getting a good night's sleep goes a long way during those times you are trying to put the past behind you. Get a good night's sleep! Then determine that when you get up, you are going to trust God about your past, and today you are going to do something fun.

Chapter 10

Endorphins and Five-Minute Facelifts

Chapter 10

Endorphins and Five-Minute Facelifts

Have you ever parted your hair down differently and gone out, to see if anyone notices? Or maybe even thrown in some highlights without telling anyone you were planning it? Changing your physical appearance is a diversionary tactic to help you forget what you were focused on the week before! When you look at yourself in the mirror and see a physical change, it helps you think, "I'm not the person I was. Look how I have changed, inside and out."

You must have frequent doses of laughter to keep the feeling of being overwhelmed at a distance.

Having spent my early college days thinking I would eventually become a neurosurgeon, I learned a lot about the human body. You have biochemical compounds in your body called endorphins. These are peptides secreted in the brain that have a pain-relieving effect like that of morphine. Certain natural foods (generally hot and spicy ones as well as chocolate) can trigger their secretion. However, people who frequently laugh have more endorphins released than those who do not have laughter in their life. God is so awesome to create such natural pain relievers within our bodies.

I have watched people come off of antidepressant medications and stabilize emotionally because they learned to lighten up and laugh a little more.

Laughter is excellent medicine, but the joy of the Lord is your strength.

_____

Plastic surgeons say that if a person smiles six to eight hours per day, he or she will *never* need a facelift. Is it any wonder that cosmetic surgery and anti-depressant pharmaceuticals are multibillion dollar industries? People have stopped smiling and laughing.

I have actually heard of mental health counselors prescribing that patients dealing with depression go rent a half-dozen comedies and watch one each night for a couple of weeks. When was the last time you laughed so hard that you could not catch your breath or tears ran down your cheeks? On the occasions this happens to me, it is almost always followed by such a big sigh and a euphoric feeling that no negative thing could touch me with a ten-foot pole.

On the few rare occasions I actually sit down in front of the television, I make a point not to watch sad dramas. Give me a comedy. Life is tragic enough by itself!

The joy that comes from pratfalls and pies in the face is no comparison to the joy of the Lord. The Scriptures teach, *"The joy of the Lord is your strength"* (Nehemiah 8:10). We can *rejoice* in our Savior, in His love, in the work He has done in our lives, and in His promises for our future. With all His overwhelming and abundant blessings, even the bad times can be filled with peace and joy that looks forward to heavenly rewards. We only pass through this life once. I am not coming back as a tree or a goat or a wheel of cheese—so, I better figure out what to do to enjoy myself on this trip. Smile, laugh—it is a free facelift and you will release those endorphins and feel better about yourself and about your life.

People who take themselves too seriously will ultimately find themselves having a hard time looking beyond other's faults and offenses. Determine today that you will not be so serious. Let the fun begin and you just might find the strength to forget the sting of pain in the midst of your joyfulness!

Chapter 11

It Is Funny to Forget
Sometimes

Chapter 11

It Is Funny to Forget Sometimes

Wouldn't it be nice if there was a controlled amnesia that steals the bad memories and leaves the good memories that give you the most strength and joy?

Sister McNeil loves people. She feels their pains deeply. She is always getting prayer cloths anointed to take to the infirm, sad, and dying. One night she had three prayer cloths anointed and prayed over in the Wednesday evening intercessory prayer service. Each one was for a different person with a different need: one for a man with a heart condition, one for a woman in the hospital, and one for her mother who was at home in pain.

The next morning, Sister McNeil called me laughing, but frantic. "Pastor, what happens if you forget which prayer cloth was for whom? Does my mother get healed of a heart condition she does not have, and does the woman in the hospital go home to be in pain?"

It is funny to forget sometimes.

Do not be embarrassed.

Let it happen.

Forgetting can be fun.

Laughter has a definite "morphine" effect. People who do not laugh at their forgetfulness get nasty and edgy as they get older.

Think about your most embarrassing moments. You pray that no one will remember your humiliation. And then one day, someone brings up the time you fell off the stage in front of the entire congregation, and it seems funny, because time allows you the ability to look back and humorously reminisce without being so hard on yourself.

Everyone has made mistakes, but God's mercies are new every morning. Great is His faithfulness!

Keep in mind that time heals a lot of wounds.

Do not make drastic judgments today based on how you feel about yesterday's mistakes. The way you perceive them now and the way you will perceive them in the years to come will be extremely different.

Years ago, as a young pastor, I wanted to do everything just right and please everyone. One evening, my wife and I had been invited to a dinner at a precious Yugoslavian family's home. Hospitality is of major importance to this family. If you enter their doors for the slightest moment, you must drink a Coke and have a kolache (a light, fruit-filled Slovakian pastry). You have no choice. "Oh, yes, you would like a Coke, and you will eat this, and here—eat some more" and so on. They are precious people who love to be hospitable.

This particular dinner was set up weeks in advance.

- Punch line = I forgot.
- Bad part = I could not even say *we* (my wife and I) forgot.
- Reason = It was a surprise for my wife.
- Result = I had an intense desire to crawl under a rock.

They called while my wife and I were eating a sandwich at home that night, and in broken English said, "You still not coming?" They had been heating and reheating dinner for *three hours*, waiting for us.

Now, as I write this book, I laugh.

Need I say more?

There are people who seem to recall only the bad moments in their lives. Without seeing the humor, they keep reliving all these "mess-ups." Eventually, their self-esteem is based on a series of embarrassments.

Here's a secret: *everyone* has made the same mistakes at one point! That's what makes us human. The good news is,

> *Through the Lord's mercies we are not consumed, because His compassions fail not. They are new every morning; Great is Your faithfulness.* (Lamentations 3:22–23 NKJV)

Each day is a fresh start.

With that in mind, time will allow you to laugh at these things that now make you cry. "This too shall pass," and it just may wind up providing you with a humorous anecdotal moment that gets you beyond other serious times.

Chapter 12

Dealing with Jerks

Chapter 12

Dealing with Jerks

People must occasionally be forgotten in order for us to retain our sanity. One day I was driving along. Things were calm. Music was on the radio. The sun was shining. I was not in any hurry. Then I encountered "the jerk." Because I was enjoying a daydream, I did not drive as fast as he apparently wanted. I noticed him when he whipped out around me, honking and gesturing to let me know that I was a living "speed bump" in his life's road. Feeling as if an intruder just broke into my most serene, private place, I immediately sped up and followed him, to really scare him instead of *just turning right and letting him go.* (It is painful to admit this was me.)

My blood pressure shot up to about 300/180. I decided to follow the "dear young man." I sped up, turned as he turned, followed him down a side street, and acted as if I were calling the police on my car phone. Suddenly, "the jerk" stopped in the middle of the road, got out of his car, and began to run back to my car window, which I quickly rolled up. He was determined to pull me out of that car. I almost became the lead story on the six o'clock news! It was then that I realized what I had *allowed* him to do to me. I never "peeled out" and away from somebody so quickly in my life! I guess God was letting me experience a dress rehearsal for this chapter.

If you try to chase every honking "jerk" on the highway of your life, you will burn out your motor much sooner than it otherwise would—not to mention that you may end up in an accident or get pummeled. You need to make up your mind that you will not leave this world even five seconds earlier due to negative emotions. I truly do believe that I have preached funerals of people who died earlier than they should have *because they refused to turn right and let the jerk go!*

While they could have been at the zoo with their child, they were wasting time chasing the "jerk." Instead, just wave and smile, turn the radio up, or stop and get a candy bar and an ice-cold soda. Do not allow yourself to waste valuable time and precious energy on folks you cannot follow through with later in order to correct their errors. Some people are just not teachable—*turn right and let them go!*

Many hurting people have difficulty in their marriages because they cannot do this. The injuries of old relationships keep cropping up. Holding on to past relationships may cause you to compare your spouse to an "ex." You may assume your spouse is going to exhibit the same reactions and create the same problems, which may not be the case. You cannot be successful in a new relationship until you release the offenses of the old. Unless you want to wind up in a self-induced psychosis, you must learn a few simple tricks.

First of all, remind yourself, "God has a plan for my life," and nobody appears in His "video" of my life unless *He* allows it—which means everyone serves a purpose in your life. Maybe he or she was teaching you to appreciate the love God has brought into your life today. Or perhaps they were being used by God to show you what happens when you become a person devoid of patience or gratitude. Take the lesson, use it, but always *turn right and let them go!*

You cannot be successful in a new relationship until you release the offenses of the old.

Friendships may fall apart, but this breach does not have to be permanent. Often two people part, maybe for years, but after maturing and realizing how badly they miss the good parts of the friendship (and if you will be honest with yourself, you will admit there were good parts), they come back together for an even stronger relationship. Relax and let time heal. Focus on what is in front of you, not what you left behind. Your reach should always be greater than your grasp.

You cannot resurrect a crushed daffodil, but do not let that keep you from smelling a blossoming lilac.

Go back to being a kid for a moment. Remember how, as children, we were more interested in playing than holding a grudge. After a day or two, or even after an hour, we just chose not to discuss disagreements anymore because we knew how to *turn right and let them go!* It's not too late to have that attitude again! A great example of this attitude is the following story.

When my son Chad was eight years old, I often heard him before I saw him. He was such an "outdoorsman." I used to think somewhere in the jungle, Tarzan was looking for his son, and I had him. Fish, bears, coyotes, dirt, worms, deer, and "unairconditioned" activities were all he dreamed of.

"Dad, I am *never* speaking to Jeff again," he cried.

"Now, son, it can't be all that bad."

"No, Dad, never, *never* again!"

His sobs grew louder.

"Chad, listen to me..."

"Dad, he *stole* my roadkill!"

Roadkill! How could this be my son, and how could roadkill be *his* anyway? As I reached down to start wiping the grime and the small collection of nature off his clothes, I asked him to explain.

Chad and Jeff, our next-door neighbor's son, were going to "play taxidermy" and stuff a squirrel that had "gone on ahead." Jeff had run off with the star of the show. Now Chad was truly heartbroken and, with great anger, had come home to get a BB gun and go find Jeff.

Have you ever had a day like that? Probably not—unless you have a son with a BB gun!

Well, after much "diversion" and, thankfully, a service to get to on time, we convinced Chad that we would settle this dispute the following day.

Life has too much to offer for you to waste a day being bitter.

As I arrived home that next day, dreading what lay ahead—there were Chad and Jeff in the lilac tree, setting "bear traps." Yesterday's traumatic roadkill incident was the furthest thing from their minds.

The adult in me still wanted to teach Jeff a lesson. But the child in my son had already chosen not to waste another minute on being estranged from his hunting partner.

Children have a tremendous ability to forgive. We "big kids" have matters of pride and territory. Jesus said, *"Except ye...become as little children, ye shall not enter into the kingdom of heaven"* (Matthew 18:3). I cannot help but believe that one of the ways in which we do this is by forgiving and forgetting.

Children have a tremendous ability to forget. One definition of *forget* is applicable here: "to fail to recall." It is active. It denotes choice. A child fails to remember or chooses *not* to recall offenses. Life has too much to offer them to let a day be wasted on bitterness.

Even though they may be justified in their contempt, they choose to erase it from the board. They will "fail to recall" for the sake of present enjoyment. They refuse to fuss about roadkill when they could be climbing lilac trees and setting bear traps.

Step away from the roadkill.

There's a lilac tree with your name on it.

Finally, brethren, whatsoever things are true, whatsoever things are honest, whatsoever things are just, whatsoever things are pure, whatsoever things are lovely, whatsoever things are of good report; if there be any virtue, and if there be any praise, think on these things.

(Philippians 4:8)

The next verse goes on to say that the God of peace will show up after you have your thinking on this track.

Chapter 13

Clueless

Chapter 13

Clueless

S ometimes people tell us these amazing stories that have happened to them, and we listen and smile, but it doesn't seem that great. We respond, "I guess you had to be there." I had a truly amazing event take place, and I hope you'll agree. Before it started, I was completely clueless to the miracle about to happen.

Actually, this day started twenty years ago. I was a twenty-five-year-old zealous and energetic young preacher. The congregation at that point was about forty or fifty people on a good Sunday. I was raised believing that door-to-door soul winning was the epitome of "proving your salt," as the old timers use to say. So, while sitting in my office and desiring to reach Chicago with ministry, I thought, "Why not start in my own neighborhood?" I promptly got up and, with Bible and tracts in hand, decided to go soul winning. I started out on foot within the blocks surrounding our church.

Several hours later I came upon a willing listener. Liz was gracious, kind, and sincerely hungry for more of God in her life. I knew it was a divine inspiration that had caused me to go from my office that day and into the line of fire to find that one lost sheep. Liz and her husband invited me into their home, and for the next few minutes, we shared one of the warmest conversations I have ever had. We talked of God's love for us and our love for Him. Before we knew it, we were all weeping. I asked if I could come back the following Monday night and teach an in-home Bible study to their family. They readily agreed. So for the next ten Monday evenings we studied God's Word together. I baptized them. I loved their family deeply. I felt like God had bound our lives together with cords that would never be violated or broken. They became the dearest people I knew. I depended on them. They depended on me. Our children grew to be friends with each other. Our hearts seemed knit as one.

> You never know what God is doing in the hearts of others. But He is working for what is best for you!

Then came the pain. They went "missing in action." For every preacher who has counted on someone to be there, the spirit of disappointment in that situation is depressing like no other. You are sure that nothing can rip apart the friendship. You know that there is such a mutual respect and love that it is indefatigable. After all, you have cried together, dined together, worshipped together, shared Christmas gifts together!

Nevertheless, they were truly missing, and I knew there was a problem. Nothing big happened; they had just lost interest. Despite wanting to mourn this broken relationship, I had to go on. I had to put on a happy face and light up the room. I had to sing, preach, and encourage others when I knew I needed it as much as anyone. But this was my calling.

During this time, I shed tears. I would call Liz or her husband in the hope that by hearing the hurt in my voice they would want to come back. Little did I know how many times this scene would repeat itself through the process of my life. Surely I could convince them differently. And the truth is, I could not. Only God can change a heart. You cannot convince someone to love you. You cannot convince someone to stay. And even if they do because of guilt, it won't last. You are only delaying the inevitable. Band-Aids® will not stop the bleeding of a wounded heart.

My middle daughter came into the room the night I had my last telephone conversation with them. I always hid my feelings pretty well about things like that, but it was the moment of impact, and I was a mess. I was crying and sobbing in pain. She was so young but realized her dad was wounded. And every child etches moments like that into his or her memory forever. It pained our family. We hurt together. And my children were, of course, set out to defend their father from any more hurt.

Fifteen years elapsed. I had learned how to go on. When the sad thoughts would come, I would do my best to suck it up. However, that is only part of the story. For Liz's story is the other half. Little did I know what God had been doing in them through that time. Guilt and sorrow began to settle into their lives. Because our parting had been so painful at the end, they dismissed the idea of patching things up. All the while, God was at work!

You never know what God is doing in the heart of the one who has abandoned you. The heart of every man is in God's hand. He can turn it however He wishes. And often He does not tell you what He is doing, let alone consult with you about what you think the outcome should be. But He is working for whatever is best for you!

> Waiting on the other side of your pain is beauty for ashes.

For fifteen years they wandered and thought, and wished and prayed. I was clueless. Sometimes you have to be clueless to stay out of God's way. We interfere way too much. We can slant things in ways that do not mend, which then create guilt and frustration that add injury to insult. So God does it without you. Amazing! He is concerned about the people who have injured you because they are still, much to our chagrin, His children even when we are in pain. He wishes for none to perish. (See Matthew 18:14.) So He just keeps molding them and making them into His plan for their lives, whether you know it, see it, or believe it. Clueless! Waiting on the other side of your pain is beauty for ashes (see Isaiah 61:3), but I had to forget it to let God fix it. I could not be a part of their journey toward our future restoration. Only God could observe both parties. What happened next is nearly impossible to conceive.

Fifteen years later my phone rang. "Could there be a way to start over again?" they asked. I could hardly believe my ears. Start over? Again? After fifteen years? But when God leads someone, He truly leads them. They were coming to Chicago and asked if we could please meet. With some apprehension, I agreed. Weeks later we would see each other for the first time in fifteen years. On a sunny, beautiful, and warm day, there we stood weeping.

It would have been enough if the story ended there, but because there is a principle of recovery involved in restoration, there is always a bonus track on God's CD player. The re-mix to your former relationships is amazing when God is the producer. And then, the bombshell came. "Pastor, God told us to sow a very specific seed into your life." They explained to me that this was a mandate from God over which I had no control, and they were doing it. They desired to be obedient. I must receive it.

I allowed God to work in my life so I could forgive these dear friends and forget the pain they had caused with me. If I had held a grudge and allowed bitterness to keep me from meeting with them that day, I never would have had the chance to accept their apology or their gift.

Most importantly, I would have missed out on a wonderful friendship and denied God's blessing in my life.

Out of the bitter comes the sweet. All of that time God had been perfecting that which was concerning me, and I was truly clueless. That day was like no other. They delivered on their promise, and I became the envy of my sixteen-year-old son who *definitely* feels God is calling me to regift and sow a specific seed into his life. Not your normal day, for sure. So now I am looking at every situation that has caused me pain over the last twenty-eight years of ministry and wondering what else God might have up His divine sleeve. Do not be discouraged and do not worry about calling, e-mailing, obsessing, or writing. God works best in our unawareness of His divine acts. When we are ready and when they are ready, something beautiful will unfold.

Pull your shoulders back, lift your head up, and speak to your emotions: "If today is as good as it is going to get, I am blessed right now. If this is as thin as I will ever be, I am blessed right now. If this is as good-looking as I will ever be, I am blessed right now. I am not waiting on my dreamboat to come in to enjoy life; I am blessed with what I currently have. In spite of what I lost that was so painful, what God left me with is so powerful."

Whether or not I know anything about what God is up to, it is okay. Silence is golden. God is working without your interference, and it will be perfect when it comes back to you.

Chapter 14

Flowers Bloom in the Strangest Places

Chapter 14

Flowers Bloom in the Strangest Places

Have you ever tried to talk to somebody about what you have gone through, only for them to categorically "one-up" everything you said with an experience of their own that was even more *fantastic* than yours?

Imagine being on a talk show with *Joseph*. He could top anyone. You picture something bad, and it probably happened to him:

- He was a victim of jealousy and hatred.
- There was a conspiracy to kill him.
- His own brothers betrayed him.
- He was kidnapped and stripped.
- He starved, knowing his captors were eating.
- He was thrown in a pit.
- He was sold as a slave.

- He was reported dead to his beloved father.
- He was lustfully and sexually preyed on by a woman.
- He was put in prison on false charges.
- After interpreting dreams in prison with only one request—that he be remembered when the king's butler got out—*he was forgotten!*
- He was promoted from prison to vice president of Egypt!
- He was the means of saving a family and a nation, through whom the Messiah would come!

Can you top Joseph?

But Joseph learned, "Life is not always fair, but God is just!"

He said to his brothers at the end of all this suffering, *"But God did send me before you to preserve life"* (Genesis 45:5).

The conditions of life will make us bitter or better.

The conditions of life will make us bitter or better.

When King David suffered all his disasters, he determined to allow suffering to produce its finished product: brokenness. He found his kingdom gone, his associates disbanded, and his greatest pain—the loss of his dearest son. He bowed to the ground, clothed in sackcloth, and anointed his head with ashes. But he *refused* to become bitter. Out of his brokenness came restoration, and because of this understanding, David was called a man after God's own heart. (See Acts 13:22.)

If you harden your heart, the effect of suffering is lost, and the lesson you were to learn from that suffering will still need to be learned at a later time. When brokenness of spirit transpires (an emptying of self facilitating an influx of God Almighty), *restoration* can begin.

I love illustrations. I just wish this one had happened to someone else, because the pain seemed to be never-ending. However, it changed my view and helped me survive suffering.

At sixteen years of age, my whole world collapsed. My parents separated and moved three hundred miles away from one another. My mother was completely devastated by the splitting of our family. Because of the events leading up to this devastation of our family unit, I began inwardly to build giant monuments of hatred to my father.

My father had never been a very affectionate man to his children to begin with, so this only fueled my fire. He had never been the "communicator" we so desperately needed him to be for us as we grew, so my bitterness bloomed into full-blown hatred.

He hurt my mother.

He hurt my family.

He hurt our reputation.

He hurt me. (Be careful of the "hurt" word. It isn't too far from "hate.")

I could not understand why he did the things he did.

Fifteen years passed.

I was trying to help others cope with their suffering. I went on talk shows as the expert special guest, wrote songs, spent untold hours counseling hurting people—all the while bitter because I could not tell my father I had needed him and that I was angry with him. Bitterness defined me, and I had told no one while attempting to help everyone else.

God showed me how painful circumstances worked for my good.

Then one day, while in a magnificent presence of the Lord during a worship service, tears began to come to my eyes. My hardened heart had blinded me to my reality. How could I have been so blind?

In my mind, I saw myself in a salvage yard, where things are sorted out after a train wreck, fire, or other disaster. I had been through a disaster, but I had not seen the good things that had been salvaged in my life, because I was staring so intently at the huge mound of "bad."

 Freedom to Forget

As I walked over to view the results of all this suffering, to my surprise I began to find the treasures (the fruit) among the wreckage. Surprises I found because of my father's actions:

- I was put into a situation where I was forced to learn responsibility while still very young. I had thought I missed out because I was unable to engage in "normal" teenage frivolity and irresponsibility. Yet, largely because of that, I had always found a way to put food on the table and hold down a job, and I had seen God "make a way out of no way" numerous times.

- I had to work, but it made me get a jumpstart on others my age. I had a good four extra years on my peers in getting established in the business world and was able to buy my first home at the age of twenty-one.

- I had been too busy working, going to college full-time, and trying to keep a church operating to get involved in gangs, drugs, or alcohol.

In my salvage yard, I saw, for the first time, fruit that was produced in my life by adverse circumstances!

I remember the first hug I gave my dad. I thanked him for what he had taught me. (Imagine his shock!) As we embraced for the first time in fifteen years, my tears fell in tandem with his.

Flowers Bloom in the Strangest Places

Things are not 100 percent yet (we are both working on it), but if you had ever told me ten years ago that I would be happy to see my father come back into our family Christmas gathering, I would have scorned your faith. When brokenness comes, restoration follows!

Beautiful flowers can still grow out of the mounds of dirt in your life. They are not looking for a perfect yard; they can grow in the most unlikely places. The quicker you recognize the fruit that suffering produces, the quicker you can move on! A Christian is like a teabag: not worth much until he or she has been through some hot water!

Chapter 15

Reconciliation Goes
a Long Way

Chapter 15

Reconciliation Goes a Long Way

In the previous chapter, I bared my heart about the story of my father and the nonexistent relationship we fostered for years, and of the pain caused not only by the damage he had done to our family, but also by my unwillingness to truly and completely forgive. Now that forgiveness has taken place and much of the reconciliation that can accompany forgiveness has happened, I find that a lot of the hurt and pain of those days no longer has an emotional stranglehold on me. I have truly begun to forget some of the incidents and the painful emotions that were so debilitating just a few years ago.

Sometimes reconciliation is not possible. Perhaps the one who offended you refuses to be a part of the process. Perhaps he or she is dead. Perhaps he or she has a life-long restraining order against you, or it would be way too inconvenient or inappropriate to make any attempt at reconciliation.

First, let me speak to those situations where reconciliation, on some level, can take place. If you can take it, reconciliation is a step beyond forgiveness, and when you are willing and able to take that step, it will go a long way to eradicating many of the painful memories of bygone days.

If the person is dead, you could go and sit at the gravesite—simply as a powerful way to reconnect with the memory of the person. There you could confess that you have forgiven them and have realized the beautiful results that God has used even this to your betterment. You could confess that you are going to let go of the past, that you are no longer going to recount the details, and that, if they were still alive, you would thank them for what their life and mistakes have taught you.

When you forgive, you can recognize valuable lessons and the way God has restored and blessed your life.

If they live some distance away, or it would be too hard to see them, you could write them a letter (assuring them no response is needed) that states not only had you forgiven them, but that you have learned valuable lessons and that God has restored and blessed your life as a result of going through those unfortunate times. Do not recount the details, and do not use the occasion to blame them for what happened.

If they are friends or fellow parishioners and you see them a lot, I have to believe that, since our God is a God of reconciliation, forgiveness, and realization, even bad things work for our benefit. God will avail you of a very good opportunity to approach them let them know that you have missed their friendship, or at least the ability to be friendly, and that not only have you forgiven them but you have truly blossomed and grown as a result of the situation.

The Bible says, *"If your brother sins against you, go and tell him his fault between you and him alone. If he hears you, you have gained your brother"* (Matthew 18:15 NKJV). God is a God of reconciliation. After all, He sent His Son to die on a cross so He could be reconciled to mankind. He can work miracles in your relationships and restore them.

Not every situation has an unburned bridge remaining for you to recross and do this reconciliation. However, if reconciliation can be accomplished (whether weeks, months, or years later) it goes along way toward helping you to forget the past and press forward.

Chapter 16

The Product of Adversity

Chapter 16

The Product of Adversity

I n 2 Corinthians 12, Paul talked about the many revelations, visions, and spiritual insights God had given him. He started out the chapter by saying that it was not right for him to boast about all that God had opened to his understanding, but then went on to discuss just a few of those things to make a point. Then in verse seven, he said that God was allowing something, an "agent" straight out of hell, to torment or agitate him. The purpose? So Paul would not get puffed up with pride over all God had revealed to him.

Paul earnestly sought the Lord many times to remove this "thing." God's only response was, essentially, "No, My grace is sufficient to be strong in the area that this 'thing' is making you weak." (See verse 9.) This passage has been transforming for me.

Recently, I have been trying to help my congregation understand that being blessed is an attitude, a privilege of God's children, not a feeling. We often repeat several times, "I am blessed right now. It is not a feeling. It is a fact!"

Is this because I do not have issues or obstacles I am facing that are almost crushing me? No, I have my own "thorns in the flesh," but each time I pray about them, I get an impression from the Lord that this thorn is just what is needed in my life to keep me prostrate before Him. It is of the utmost importance that I daily stay before Him in order to not be sidetracked into bitterness, anger, or resentment. Offenses will come, but as I love the Lord and understand His Word, I am to let nothing cause me to stumble. (See Psalm 119:165.)

Paul's trials and failures were transforming things in his life to keep him from an eternity apart from God.

Recently, an elder within our congregation confirmed this during our men's prayer group. After praying, we normally have a round of testimonies as well as prayer requests. He was praising God for the "hell" in his life, for the trials and failures, which he confessed were almost completely his own doing. However, he knew that through them God was transforming things in his life to keep him from an eternity apart from God. In other words, God was using the torment of his failures to establish in him the right attitude, a mind of faith, and a heart filled with love and worship toward God—which will keep him from ever hearing the words, *"I never knew you"* (Matthew 7:23). Isn't that what it is all about?

Often, one of the big reasons we are unable to let go of the pain, sadness, and sorrow of offenses committed against us is that we do not see how God is going to use *even that* to make us more reliant upon Him and more pliable to His strength flowing through our lives. As I have looked back at some of the most painful moments in my life, I have discovered times of intimate prayer and seeking God for understanding, healing, and forgiveness. Through those times I grew remarkably closer to God; I understood more about His plans for my life and the power of His grace to keep me even through adversity. That same elder said this: "God did not just wake up today and realize what happened to you, and now He has to develop a whole new plan for you. He saw it coming and is going to use even this to your benefit—ultimately even to keep you out of an everlasting hell."

Do you want to learn how to forget? Grasp the concept that even the offense and the painful consequences that follow are but speed bumps to slow us down, detour signs keeping us from bridges that are out ahead, and traffic delays on the highway of life that may have just saved us from a fatal accident. It is easy to let go of other's abrasiveness, rudeness, and cruelty when you realize God just used them to knock off some of the rough edges you had, rough edges that may have caused others debilitating damage that may have kept you out of a whole new level of intimacy with God.

Chapter 17

Discover Your Purpose

Chapter 17

Discover Your Purpose

It is impossible to dwell on the past if you have purpose in your life!

I have heard a lot of people quote Romans 8:28 incompletely. They put the emphasis on *"And we know that **all things work together for good** to them that love God..."* Hang on! It ends with: *"...to them who are the called **according to his purpose**."*

Webster's New World Dictionary defines *purpose* as: "to intend, resolve, or plan" and to do it with "the end goal in view."

It is not just ask and receive, name it and claim it, blab it and grab it, or, as some preachers purport, "Just reach up and take it!" You must have purpose ahead to get over the past and not just any purpose, but God's purpose—your calling—the fulfillment of the will of God in your life.

God's number one agenda is the salvation of souls! Quit waiting for the right church, the right conditions, the right time, a better pastor, more friends—start today on getting involved somehow in God's agenda. People who do not know God's will for their lives, and are always seeking somebody to give them a word about it, are not involved in God's agenda!

You must get involved in God's agenda to find your purpose.

Why are there dozens of talk shows on television and even more radio talk shows? Smut and gutter talk is where it begins, and it goes down from there, yet these talk show hosts are millionaires.

They have an audience.

Why do they have an audience?

Because people have no purpose. They know something is missing, and they are looking for anything to fill the void.

Why do some people always seem prone to "throwing in the towel"? They have no purpose! They are not involved in any acts of soul winning.

I just visited a small church that has had no growth in the last twenty years at all. These people all practically hate one another. Fighting, feuding—how they have church, I do not know! But it dawned on me how many of their problems we have had in our own church. *I had forgotten them.* You know why? Because we never even had a chance to settle them. We did not have time to dwell on them. We had too many new babies being born again who needed our attention.

Churches that are not about God's purpose (winning souls) will end up fighting one another just to have something to do. Remember hell and the devil are after you every day, but they cannot stop you if you have purpose! *"We are troubled on every side, yet not distressed; we are perplexed, but not in despair;*

God's agenda will help you find your purpose or niche in life.

persecuted, but not forsaken; cast down, but not destroyed" (2 Corinthians 4:8–9). These things happen in our lives so when the vibrant life of God shows up and brings peace, our familiars look on and say, "Wow, where do you get this peace?"

You will not have time to sweat the small stuff if you are seeking God's will and purpose in your life.

It is a proven fact: people who keep working, even after retirement, doing something that challenges them, live longer. You are like an airplane: if you stop, you drop.

Do you want to surprise everyone you know—and maybe yourself? Show up for bus ministry this Saturday, or ask the pastor for a list of visitors he needs help calling so you can invite them back to church.

Get focused.

Get a purpose.

The past will release you if you find your purpose for the future, and you just might find that God has used even those past offenses to teach you invaluable lessons about how to proceed in that purpose!

Chapter 18

Dysfunctional Families

Chapter 18

Dysfunctional Families

I came from a dysfunctional family," she said to me through her sobbing. This was an expression I had already heard several times in the early 90s, but was beginning to hear more and more. Little did I realize just how many times that statement would be proclaimed in the years to come. I looked at her and said, "You know, come to think of it, you are in good company, because I currently have no one in my life that I know of who did *not* come from a dysfunctional family."

There is so much pain and suffering in homes today. *You* have undoubtedly had grief of some kind—an abusive father, an overbearing mother, a neglectful mate, a rebellious child, a divorce, the loss of a loved one, disrespect from someone in authority over you. There are a vast numbers of possible mechanisms by which life's wounds can be inflicted.

Charles Swindoll says that only 10 percent of what we experience in life is what happens to us; the other 90 percent is our response. You probably have little or no control over the 10 percent that comes your way, but you do have control over the 90 percent (your reactions).

No one can *forget* who does not *forgive*. Have you ever heard or said, "Well, I will forgive you, but I will *never* forget what you did"?

There are three things you need to do to overcome that debilitating thinking.

- First, stop speaking that!

You are building a monument to bitterness that will require your constant attention to maintain. You will have to polish up the details, replay the words, and visualize their expressions again and again. Instead, allow the details to become vague.

- Second, you must make sure that, as you forgive, you also release that person from guilt.

Until you release them from guilt, you will not be released from guilt yourself, because if you sow to the wind, you will reap the whirlwind. (See Hosea 8:7.)

Making a person who has offended you feel guilty only keeps the flaming embers of unforgiveness red hot. I once heard someone say, "Unforgiveness is like a burning ember that you want to hurl at the person who hurt you; the longer you hold it, the more it burns you." Guilt requires "mega" energy, and sending someone on a guilt trip involves a lot of work:

There's the packing: "What expression should I wear?"

Then there are the arrangements: "What will I say to them?"

Finally, there are all the travel agents: people all too willing to help map it out.

> The Holy Spirit is the only prescription for loosing bondage brought on by having had a "dysfunctional family."

Turn the guilt trips into an all-expense-paid cruise on the ship called *Liberty*. People who bask in the Spirit of the Lord seldom bind others with guilt or are bound with guilt.

If you allow yourself to marinate in the Spirit of God long enough and often enough, the rotten smell of guilt will be replaced with the beautiful aroma of liberty! Even Satan must be silent in the presence of the Spirit of God! Because *"where the spirit of the Lord is, there is liberty"* (2 Corinthians 3:17).

Focus on the blood of Jesus. That is what gives you the power to release. You are right: you cannot do it, but the Spirit of God in you can! First John 1:7 is written in the present (continuing) tense, *"The blood of Jesus...cleanses us from all sin"* (NKJV). It is continually as powerful as when it was splattered on an old rugged cross two thousand years ago! All guilt, whether given or received, will bow to the blood of Jesus.

• Third, start speaking it out loud.

Tell the devil, tell yourself, tell your family and friends, and remind God, confessing openly, "I will overcome this and forget the pain, because of the blood of Jesus and the word of my testimony." (See Revelation 12:11.)

The Spirit of God is the only prescription for loosing bondage brought on by having had a "dysfunctional family." As a child of God, you have been adopted into His family and are now one of His heirs, and He is not a dysfunctional father!

Chapter 19

Just Going through the Cemetery

Chapter 19

Just Going through the Cemetery

I remember telling my child psychology professor in college that the following statement could not be true: "A child needs attention, and he will obtain it one way or the other. If he cannot get it by being good, he will be bad just to get attention." Now, as the father of four children (the youngest of whom is now sixteen and just started driving), I *completely* concur. In the mind of a child, negative attention is better than no attention.

Sometimes in this journey of life, we hang on to past pain because we see no light in front of us. Therefore, it is something to hold on to; something to talk about is better than nothing!

That light you need to help you forget is hope!

Everybody needs hope. If you are still breathing, there is hope!

One mother was able to visit her only son's grave because she engraved hope on his tombstone: "He's not gone—He's just gone on ahead."

Some people have a special gift for taking hope away. Your child has a rash you are trying to get rid of. Those "Job's comforters" say, "It is probably the same problem my little Billy had. The dermatologist cost me sixty dollars; the medication cost me a hundred eighty-five, and *to this very day,* he is not the same."

They snatch your hope with a look, a word, an opinion.

If you were to tell someone: "The preacher said that my cup will be full and running over," they would probably respond, "You're going to need a mop to clean that up with."

They disguise themselves as "realists." A realist is a person who concerns himself only with the facts as they are known to him and never with things as they might be; plainly speaking, a realist is often someone who refuses to believe things just might get better.

If I am dying and my choices of visitors are a realist or a "dreamer" who is full of hope, please send me the dreamer!

The Word of God is filled with people who learned to hold on to encouragement. There was David, who said, "My hope is in the Lord" (Psalm 130:5); Solomon who told us, *"The righteous hath hope in his death"* (Proverbs 14:32); and Abraham who, against all odds, believed in God—clinging to His promise of a son despite the unlikelihood of the fulfillment of that promise. (See Hebrews 11:17–19.)

- Your life isn't what you expected. Is there breath? There's hope.

- Gangs, racism, hatred. Is there a church? There's hope.

- A child beaten, neglected, abused, and demoralized. Is there a weeping Sunday school teacher? There is hope.

- A broken spirit, dashed by an abusive spouse and abandoned to four small rooms of life. Is there an intercessor in the house? There is hope!

If your only associates and friends are those who are somber, sad, and validating your despair, find yourself some new friends. Laugh with some new faces.

I've heard that hope is like changing a baby's diaper. It doesn't permanently solve any problem, but it makes things more tolerable for a while.

But I say that hope is an attitude that can completely revolutionize the way you live. Refuse to allow anyone to deplete your hope. For those who have lost a loved one, here's a true story to give you some hope.

A widower in the 1940s took the streetcar home late every evening. His wife had passed on, and he was left to care for four children. He had arranged his schedule so that he could be with his children every morning to get them off to school, and then he would head to work on the streetcar. This made him return home late in the evening. His nightly exit from the streetcar was observed for several weeks by a young man riding that same car. He noticed the gentleman getting off at the cemetery every evening, even though it was dark by this time. Finally, his curiosity overcame him, and he asked the conductor, "Sir, do you know why that man gets off the streetcar every night and goes to the cemetery?" The kind conductor motioned for him to come over to the side. "See that little light flickering across the way? Well, that's where that man lives, and the cemetery is his quickest way home. Son, he is not going to the cemetery; he is just going through the cemetery!"

Hope is an attitude that can completely revolutionize the way you live.

Remember, *"If we who are [abiding] in Christ have hope only in this life and that is all, then we are of all people most miserable and to be pitied"* (1 Corinthians 15:19 AMP). Cling to hope. You will be reunited with your loved ones! They have not gone *to* the cemetery; they have just gone *through* the cemetery!

Chapter 20

No Wastebaskets in Heaven

Chapter 20

No Wastebaskets in Heaven

"I will never get over this!"
"You are always going to be that way!"
"I have said it a million times!"

We are such people of extremes, and we use such excessive phraseology that projects such drastic pictures.

"Big" is no longer descriptive enough. It has to be a "humongous" steak or "mile-high" pie. The speaker was not "long winded": he spoke "forever," and you thought he would "never" stop.

Extremes.

Hypercharged adjectives.

That kind of all-or-nothing thought process makes goal-setting a daunting prospect. When you are *really* struggling to get over something or someone, it is easy to feel overwhelmed—as if relief will "never" come.

Back up.

Start small.

Set minor goals for today.

"Do not bite off more than you can chew" was one of the resounding instructions of my mother.

Maybe you are overwhelmed about the prospect of never remarrying—when you are not even venturing out of the house yet.

Back up.

Perhaps you should start with setting a few small goals leading up to the goal of finding a new mate. Even better, work on yourself to be complete and whole, and trust God to bring you someone in His timing.

Or if you have lost a loved one to death, rather than speaking that you will *never* get over it or that "I have to have someone else by next year," make a few minor goals to get through today or this week.

Most people in pain cannot think about next week or even tomorrow. Pain is usually so acute that you need to know how to get through today.

Break it down:

• By 10:00 a.m. today, I am going to cry out all the tears I can.

- By 11:00 a.m., I am going to take a warm shower and put the tears away until tomorrow.

- By 12:00 p.m., I am going to comb my hair, put on my clothes, and be presentable.

- By 3:00 p.m., I am going to start lunch.

- By 4:30 p.m., I am going to have eaten a little something, if for no other reason than to get into some disciplined behaviors that will get me through today.

Minor goals, but concrete steps that make you feel you have accomplished something so you can see progress.

Goals keep you motivated for growth and help you forget the heartbreak of the past.

The darkest days are when you have nothing to look forward to. Plan a trip for *next* summer, but start with little goals *today*.

Try, "I will pass up the dessert at dinner tonight, because by next summer, I want to have this weight off," instead of, "I have to lose twenty pounds by next Friday; anyone know a good liposuctionist?"

Goals motivate.

Goals encourage.

Goals focus us.

Goals keep you putting one foot in front of the other.

The only way people can forget the pain or heartbreak of the past is to have a fresh goal to strive for. The only way people *stay* motivated for growth to any degree is to constantly set new goals when the last ones are complete.

Start with finishing one thing you have neglected.

Always remember, there is no waste with God.

He is the Ultimate Recycler.

> Remember, there is no waste with God. He's the Ultimate Recycler.

What may seem like time lost to you is only preparation for Him. He squeezes glory out of every one of life's circumstances, and there is no way He will let *anything* happen to you that will be wasted. I have seen Him make some beautiful lives, using what appeared to be only leftover fragments.

When goals become a focus, you will find that hurts and pains move down the priority list. Not only that but the achieving of them (another reason it is important to set more realistic baby step goals) does a lot to encourage us and give us hope to move beyond the despair of yesterday's tragedy.

The prodigal son found that only the Father can take what had been "wasted" and:

- Replace it

- Renew it

- Recover it

- Redeem it

- Repair it

- Relieve it

- Repay it

- Revive it

- Resolve it

- Return it

He is a God of restoration!

Chapter 21

Do Not Lie about the Pain

Chapter 21

Do Not Lie about the Pain

H ave you ever seen a brute man with a bleeding cut, and you say, "Oooh, yuck!" and he says, "What?"

You say, "Are you all right?"

And the macho man replies, "Oh, that doesn't even hurt!"

Blood means pain.

It is *abnormal*.

Something has been ripped open or severed.

Something has been destroyed.

Emotional pains are harder to spot, and people lie and hide them every day. Instead of finding healing, they pretend it doesn't hurt. Why do we say it does not hurt when it does? Especially men. Why do we feel compelled to tell others, "It doesn't bother me"?

For three reasons:

Do Not Lie about the Pain

1. Pride

Pride refers to an excessive belief in one's own worth or *self-superiority*. We do not want anyone to know we were so vulnerable that something penetrated our lofty position.

That really is not a sign of being "deep," but one of shallowness.

I am not suggesting that you want to find a good publicist and send out press releases about your pain, loss, or the problems you are experiencing. However, it is okay to find *someone* to whom you can concede your vulnerability—someone who will take it to prayer with you, not to the morning news.

A psychologist in my congregation once told me he often felt like a "high-priced friend" to people. There was often nothing he could suggest or tell people to do, but there was a release in their just knowing that they could lower their pride and talk to him about their emotions without worrying about being exposed.

You can save yourself seventy-five dollars or more an hour!

Let go of your pride and tell somebody you trust, "It hurts, and it hurts like crazy!" Then *do not* tell the next three people the same thing.

2. Admission of defeat

Remember in grade school gym class when you missed the hoop, and all the little kids said, "Ha ha, you missed. You loser!"

That is probably where it began.

You may not have realized it, but something in you "clicked" and said, "If I ever miss again, you will be the last one to know it."

We hate for people to think of us as a "loser," even when we lose. That is where excuses are birthed. So, we try to always project that "it does not bother me."

You can't do it without God's help. Put Him in charge.

Relax. Everyone loses sometimes.

It is the process of life.

And you rip the wind out of the devil's sails when you beat him to the punch line and you say to God, *"I cannot do this without You!"*

Do it now, quickly, before Satan points his bony finger in your face and says, "You cannot do it." You can say to him, "Tell me something I don't know. I have already admitted my defeat, my failure, my sin, my pain to the Lord, and now He is the one in charge—talk to Him about it!"

3. Risks

There are many things we don't want to risk, such as our reputations, experiencing unnecessary pain and loss, or losing our chance to be friends with the "cool" people.

We remember the risk from gym class that wound up in defeat. So we bit our lip or put our finger in our mouth and sucked on blood, as we said, "It doesn't bother me."

Sometimes God allows pruning to occur in our lives to help us become stronger, and when you come through this process of forgiving and forgetting, you want to at least be strong.

So take the risks.

Risk takers become presidents, preachers, and successful businessmen and women. You will never know what kind of distance you can long jump until you land in the sand trying to catapult yourself farther than the last time.

If you lose a friend because you risked being transparent, you may have to wonder about the depth of their devotion anyway. Do not let Satan tell you that there is no one left you can take that risk with. *"A man that hath friends must show himself friendly"* (Proverbs 18:24). (And, by the way—it is worth the risk. Risk-taking builds bridges over many troubled waters.)

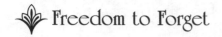

Resist the temptation to lie, because honesty will speed you along the process of *"forgetting those things which are behind, and reaching forth unto those things which are before"* (Philippians 3:13).

Everyone has pain in their lives. If they tell you that's not the case, they're lying. When we open up about the things that have hurt us, we see that others have had similar experiences. Sometimes, just knowing that can lessen the burden. Often, we can also learn from others. When you can say, "That happened in my life, and here's how I dealt with it," God may be using you to teach someone the lesson you struggled to learn, saving them additional pain.

Chapter 22

Love Checkup

Chapter 22

Love Checkup

"The only thing in life that continues to be nothing until it is given away is love."

Before you skip this and write it off as "fluff," just stop and ask yourself how you are doing on this subject.

It is time to play "Love Checkup." (Cue the theme song as the host enters stage right.)

Most of us are too self-centered and self-absorbed, which makes forgetting anything a bigger job than it should be. I used to say to my wife, Linda, about a certain lady who had a perpetual need for counseling, "Why does she keep bugging me so much? It is always about me, me, me. We keep going over her same problems."

I was becoming very resentful until I realized that in all my counseling with her, *I* was acting as an enabler to her creating a self-encompassing, self-generating cocoon. We focused every discussion on *her* phobias, *her* past, and *her* situations. *I was not steering her to others,* and a person who is not connected to others has a very difficult time moving forward.

Consider today's computerized generation and the watch word of the decade—Internet. People turn on their computers to get "connected"—the mutual exchange of information. Years ago, they would make contacts at social gatherings and parties; now we network via a computer screen. You can be connected with someone on the other side of the globe in moments. Someone is *very* rich from this bright idea, because so much can be accomplished just by bringing people together.

> How much could be accomplished if the world would come together in a holy alliance?

If the devil could build the tower of Babel with an unholy alliance—so much so that even God said there was nothing impossible for them to accomplish—then what could the people of God do in our world today if we would come together for a *holy* alliance? Homes would be restored, churches would reopen, and pastors would be encouraged. Anytime people come together and focus on the needs of others, something powerful will happen. It is a sure win.

If you are really sincere about wanting to forget, you must get on the "spiritual internet." You must get

connected to God's family. Go back to church, and place yourself under a ministry that is attempting to reach out to others!

In reaching out to others, you are absolutely going to encounter someone who is in worse condition than you. This will (a) cause you to praise God that your situation is not worse than it is and will (b) create the healing balm of love that the other person needs—which will inevitably water your parched spirit as you give it away.

How we Christians need that spiritual Internet! Has there ever been a time when you went to church, feeling blue, lonely or depressed, and someone came up to you—just shook your hand or gave you a hug and shared the love of God with you? That little bit of connection can make all the difference in the world to someone in pain. Sometimes I have received nothing more than a warm smile given to me across a crowded room, which made me feel that I was loved, respected, and appreciated, and enabled me stand a little taller.

Staying connected creates accountability. And while on the surface you may feel disdain about accountability, successful people know it breeds integrity and progress. The Bible says, *"In the multitude of counselors there is safety"* (Proverbs 11:14; see also Proverbs 24:6).

Almost every Saturday morning, at 8 a.m., for the last fifteen years, you can find me in our men's prayer group. I wish I could explain the strength I have gained from being connected to godly, praying men. On the few occasions I had to be absent, they always inquired. They did not do it with a "beat-you-up" mentality, but with a love that says, "God is using you too much for us not to form a hedge around you and protect you." Each brother in that prayer group gets:

- The feeling of being needed (and we all crave that)
- The genuine concern that you are covered in any situation
- The loving friendship for life
- The camaraderie of men of valor gathering their strength before heading into battle

All by just staying connected!

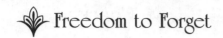

Sometimes you just need somebody
To comfort you with a smile.
Sometimes we need one another
To go that extra mile.
But we all need somebody
To show us we can make it.
God give you the courage
To heal the pain they're feeling.
Oh, reach out, friend
Share the true meaning of love.

"We All Need Somebody" words and music Rev. Dan Willis from *Live in Kingston Jamaica—We All Need Somebody!* By Rev. Dan Willis & the Pentecostals of Chicago, ©1997, Tyscot, Inc.

Chapter 23

The Chapter You May Not Want to Read

Chapter 23

The Chapter You May Not Want to Read

M aybe you are unable to forget because you are still jealous. No one knows, but *you* know it is jealousy. You could never admit it to anyone else, but it is. That's cool. You do not have to admit it to anyone other than God and yourself, but in order to quit looking back over your shoulder at that person, you are going to have to move beyond jealousy. Jealousy precludes forgiveness. It is cruel! Its victims are slaves to torment.

I once pastored a lady who had been "done wrong" by some other people. Rather than forgiving the incident and letting it go, she became consumed with blocking the "perpetrators" from getting ahead of her in any way. She became (and this is not overstating it) insanely jealous. I observed with growing dismay that the combination of the emotional injury she had sustained at the hands of these people and the jealousy that began to grow in her were the perfect components for a time bomb that was sure to explode in her at some point. One of the great ironies of the situation was that I am not completely sure the "offenders" had intended to hurt her or even realized that they had. She was the one who was being ravaged by this jealousy coupled with her unforgiveness.

If they got a new sweater, she was so obsessed with "what they had done to her" that she would talk about their sweater and go buy a sweater for herself to satisfy the demands of her all-consuming jealousy.

I pleaded with her to let it go. She denied the existence of a problem. I pleaded again. She was so close to perfect in every other

> Until you forgive, the other person controls you.

area of life—she prayed, she gave, she sang in the choir, she helped wherever needed, but because she chose not to forgive and forget as soon as the offense occurred, that cruel villain jealousy found a beautiful home to reside in.

She died in her fifties. I remember preaching her funeral and grieving, because she really *was* a precious soul, but she had allowed this jealousy to eat her life away. I believe she died before her time.

Solomon, the wisest man, said, *"Love is strong as death; **jealousy is cruel as the grave**, the coals thereof are coals of fire, which hath a most vehement*

flame" (Song of Solomon 8:6, emphasis added). You will not survive a street fight with that gangbanger called jealousy.

Until you forgive, that person continues to control you. Though you may not have seen them for years, you are still having bad days because of them. They will control you until you forgive.

When somebody says something mean to you at 9 a.m. and you have not forgiven them by 3 p.m., and you are still rehearsing how you should have told them off as you are lying in bed, they have ruined and controlled your whole day. Forgiveness enables you to take back control.

Plead now for the blood of Jesus to be applied over your ex-husband's new wife, that teenage friend who hurt you twenty years ago, or the person two rows behind you at church. Declare, "I will not go to a cold grave one day early because of *jealousy*." Jealousy helps you remember offenses, not forget them. Declare, "I am free from jealousy and the need for vengeance in the name of Jesus Christ!"

Chapter 24

Follow-Up Therapy

Chapter 24

Follow-Up Therapy

D o we not all know that "settled" does not always mean *settled*? Unfortunately, there are times along the way when we have to settle decisions again. Remember, we talked earlier about making the decision to forget and coaching ourselves until the feeling comes later? This is a choice. Occasionally, along the path of time, a song, a photo, or a name will come along that will unsettle your choice.

It is at that time you have to do follow-up therapy! This takes discipline! *Discipline* means "a training that develops self-control, character, or orderliness and efficiency; treatment that corrects."

1. Remember that you made a decision to go forward.

2. If you slip, do not slide all the way back.

3. Immediately recommit your decision to God.

4. Confess (loudly, if you must), "I am *not* taking this anxiety back on! I have already cast it on the One who can handle it!"

5. Bless someone. Remember faith without works is dead. Do something dutiful, "a cut above" for someone.

6. Practice a diversion. For instance, go to the mall and window shop; spend some time with a senior citizen who doesn't get out much, volunteer for your favorite organization, or start a hobby. In other words, get your mind "unglued."

7. Set a time limit for crying.

8. Recheck your goals, and inch toward one of them.

9. Log onto that "Christian Internet" to network with others who have *purpose* and *hope*.

10. Do not try to figure God out all at once. He has been working on it all for thousands of years.

11. As soon as you can, laugh again. Again, laughter produces a survival secretion called "endorphins" that are God's built-in pep pills. Do whatever you must to remember to enjoy life, whether that means reading a joke book, watching a comedian, or standing on your head.

12. Give a praise report to someone about God's goodness.

13. Sing. As long as it isn't "your" song, you can't stay upset when you're belting out your favorite tune and dancing around the house.

14. Stay focused on the blessings in your life, not the sufferings.

15. Confess verbally, *"I forgive."*

That might be all, if you do not have to see that person ever again. However, in God's infinite goodness and awesome wisdom, He will probably give you the opportunity to indeed see them again. Maybe they are family, go to the same church, or their child is in the same grade as your child and plays the same three sports. At the moment of encounter, with your face flushed, heart racing as the hot adrenalin rush starts pumping through your veins—screaming *fight or flight*—and your mind starts questioning how this could be happening since you settled this already, take just this little bit of advice:

You have forgiven when you can genuinely bless the other person.

1. Guide the conversation into very shallow waters (the weather, traffic, etc.); do not allow it to get heavy or confrontational.

2. Keep it as brief as possible.

3. Do not ask questions, and resist the urge to bring up the original betrayal or argument.

The quickest way to become unsettled again is to get rattled, so be classy but not aloof, humble not arrogant, cordial but not shut-down. Then as soon as you are away, genuinely bless them. In the next chapter, you will learn how to do this, but this is all an effective part of the follow-up therapy, whereby you will find yourself aspiring to put behind what happened in the past, and pressing forward toward the treasure of being more Christlike with all the blessings that accompany that.

Chapter 25

What Eagles and Your Adversary Have in Common

Chapter 25

What Eagles and Your Adversary Have in Common

P eople who you want to forget are always the hardest ones to forget. There are people in life who get gratification in knowing that they have an emotional hold on someone else. You *want* to forget them, but you are related to them, or perhaps they are your boss or someone else whom you cannot eliminate from the repertoire of people in your life. What you *must* know is that, if they are being gratified by making you anxiety-ridden by their laziness, bad humor, body odor, or general attitude, it only makes their hold deeper if you do not follow the scriptural admonition for this situation. So, if you want their hold on you to release, consider the following:

An eagle swoops down when it spots its prey—while traveling at speeds of seventy-five to one hundred miles per hour. It hits its target very hard, often stunning it, and then digs its claws in with approximately one thousand pounds of pressure per square inch in each talon until they "lock up." The mighty bird will then fly—with its talons clenching its helpless "dinner guest"—to its perch on a mountain or ledge, where the eagle will literally have to wait anywhere from ten minutes to several hours for its grip to release before it is able to eat its prey. The muscles in those powerful talons lock so completely as to make escape impossible for the victim, and the eagle is instinctively unable to loosen its grip until it feels the life and resistance drain from its captive.

When someone you do not especially care for has a grip on you to the point that you dread even seeing them—so much so that you make up excuses to avoid any contact—they are controlling you. It is not "them" we can change—it is you.

The more you wrestle against them or fight back, even by cringing or not speaking, the more you make that "eagle" dig its claws in deeper. The more you fight to get loose, the more intense their control will seem.

However, relax, and they will release.

You can release their hold on you by taking Matthew 5:44 out of print and putting it into action: *"Bless them that curse you, do good to them that hate you, and pray for them which despitefully use you."*

Bless them?

I know it is hard, but you want to be free, right?

Well, bless them!

I have discovered that this is quite possibly the most powerful weapon we have in our arsenal to forget those things which are behind. (See Philippians 3:13.)

The first act God performed after completing creation was to bless Adam and Eve. Then He made a covenant with them. Over five hundred times in the Scriptures we find the Lord giving His blessing. We are most familiar with: *"The Lord bless thee, and keep thee"* (Numbers 6:24), and *"The blessing of the Lord makes one rich, and He adds no sorrow with it"* (Proverbs 10:22 NKJV).

It is hard to bless the person who hurt you, but the Bible commands that you do so.

The blessing also played a major part in Jewish cultural events such as weddings, bar mitzvahs, and in times of birthright pronouncements, when there was transference of wealth and heritage between generations. Also, the manner in which the blessing plays a central role in everyday Jewish life is remarkable and may contribute to why there is a pattern of blessing and prosperity among many Jews.

Not everyone can give a blessing, and not everyone can bless you. The authority to give a blessing was and is a birthright privilege to all who keep covenant with God. The Scriptures tell us whatsoever things we bind or loose on earth is so done in heaven. (See Matthew 18:18.)

You might ask, what has this to do with forgiveness and learning to forget the hurt and pain of offenses endured? I am glad you asked.

In chapters twenty-five and twenty-seven of Genesis, we read how Jacob horribly wronged his brother Esau. Years later, as Jacob and all his posterity and wealth were returning to the land of Abraham and Isaac, Jacob was told that Esau was coming out to meet him with four hundred soldiers in tow. Jacob assumed, perhaps quite correctly, Esau was coming to exact his revenge. To appease Esau, Jacob sent blessings (accompanied by not just a few expensive gifts) in waves before him when he was on the way to meet Esau. By the time Esau finally met up with Jacob, he had been appeased and was willing to forget the offenses of the past.

You will know that you have truly begun to forget the sting and pain of the hurts you have forgiven when you are able to allow God to compel your heart to bless them that have despitefully used you and who may be still trying to hold you in their clutches.

Thus, the blessing serves as a release of the need for vengeance. I submit that you cannot desire and honestly pray for a blessing over someone you are

still harboring anger toward or currently desiring vengeance upon. Blessing those who have persecuted you releases you into the realm of miraculous healing from past hurts. If you need something to motivate you, let me tell you that blessing someone who has harmed you is more for your sake! It releases you out of that eagle's clasp! Actually, you never act more like a child of God than when you bless others.

"But, pastor, you do not understand what they did to me." No, dear one, you are probably right, but I have jumped on the clue-bus and been around the block just a few times and seen the destruction that abuse, neglect, and even expectations that were too high have done to folks. You do not pastor for twenty-nine years and not get your fair share of people unfairly lying about you (and your wife, and your kids and maybe even your dog) as well as straight-out trying to do you harm!

Take a look at the pattern our Lord established on the cross: though He was rejected by all men—even those closest to him—yet He prayed for a blessing that they would be forgiven and not be held accountable. As He stated, they really did not know what they were doing. (See Luke 23:34.)

Merriam-Webster's Dictionary defines *bless* as "invoke divine care for" and "to confer prosperity or happiness upon." Spiritually speaking, it is to speak forth God's favor and goodness upon another. When you finally allow yourself to be enabled by the Spirit of God to pray for and speak a blessing over those who have injured you, you have taken, if not the final step, at least a very significant one toward *"forgetting those things which are behind."*

Find a small way to compliment them—maybe about their new car, their job, their child, or even a shirt they have on. In doing so, their grip on your emotions, which they may not even realize exists, will begin to release.

The more you bless them and pray for them privately, the more that bondage is openly broken. The eagle's grasp instinctively loosens, and you are set free to begin forgetting.

Chapter 26

Get Away

Chapter 26

Get Away

I had finished writing this when I discovered one more way to help you forget. Every now and then you must get away. I am not talking about an expensive cruise or exotic vacation. It can be as simple as a drive through the forest preserve. But get out of concrete and shopping malls, meetings, carpools, and PTA agendas, and get close to nature!

I am a city boy through and through. My idea of roughing it is a double bed instead of a king-size bed at the Holiday Inn. I am not geared for the *au naturel* life. However, I discovered, as I sit here in the beautiful Upper Peninsula of Michigan, that hearing the birds sing each morning, watching deer come to the pond, and squirrels jump from tree to tree, something is transferred into my spirit. My shoulders relax (eventually), the race going on inside subsides, and the conditions are right for "forgetting it all."

Even Jesus had to "come aside." (See Matthew 14:23 and Mark 6:31.) Surely we must—if for no other reason than to step back from your own disasters to realize that the world is bigger than your little portion—and it is all in order. No phones, televisions, or schedules. Just peace.

When was the last time you removed your self from all the ringing phones, screaming sirens, washing machines, and radios, and took a short walk through God's magnificent creation?

There is something so deep about realizing there are opportunities outside of your four walls. The sun does shine in other places. You will be able to come back with a renewed strength and vigor from taking a break.

> When you need to replenish, take advantage of God's creation.

Even a powerfully built bodybuilder gets weak after working out because his muscles fatigue. This does not mean that he is weak; it just means he has been pressing, straining, and even causing micro-tears in the muscles. Those muscles need to renew, replenish, and heal. Even a short break will let him do more and push farther than he thought possible. So, take the time to stop and smell the honeysuckle—or roses if that is your favorite!

Relax. Go do it.

You will create the proper conditions and atmosphere for your mind to be able to forget.

 Freedom to Forget

Why should I feel discouraged?
Why should the shadows come?
Why should my heart feel lonely
And long for heaven and home?
When Jesus is my Portion,
A constant Friend is He.
His eye is on the sparrow,
And I know He watches me.

I sing because I'm happy.
I sing because I'm free.
His eye is on the sparrow,
And I know He watches me!

"His Eye Is on the Sparrow" words by Civilla Martin, music by Charles H. Gabriel, 1905.

Chapter 27

Turn the Lights On

Chapter 27

Turn the Lights On

I was raised in religious paradigm where standards of excellence and performance were a part of securing a good standing with God. We did not wear some things, go some places, and attempted to stay as far away from the religious boundaries we had established for ourselves in order to own a feeling of being loved and accepted by God. I have many memories of feeling "beaten up" by that approach to living for God, and I saw many others beaten up and run off.

Today, to distance myself from the very negative aspects of that style of approach to God, I have taken the approach that mine is not the place to beat you up, but rather to "turn on the lights for you." If it illuminates things in your life that you need to dispense with, I believe you will take the necessary actions to access the grace and help of God to dispose of those things.

As I conclude I want to repeat the sum of the matter, as Solomon once said when concluding Ecclesiastes. I want to turn on the lights one last time, by reminding you of what we have covered:

- *"Brothers, I do not consider myself yet to have taken hold of* [perfection]. *But one thing I do: forgetting what is behind and straining toward what is ahead... I press on toward the goal"* (Philippians 3:13–14 NIV).

- There *is* a way to let go of hurts! It *can* be done! So, cry until He tells you, "Let it go. Let it be." Cry until the revelation of "Your will is what is best for me..."[2] assuages the grief. Lean not on your own understanding, but rather lean upon God's comforting presence as you lament and purge your heart of the pain. You will go on—you will learn to forget!

- Then, cry a little more, not tears of self-sympathy, but of further release. "Dear God, I cannot do this without you; please take it, take it *all*—and please take it now." Then, when you have given it to God, your eyes are tired, your mind emptied, and your emotions spent, you can sleep peacefully. Be assured thatbthe sun will shine in the morning!

- Determine to never be bitter at God and grab for excuses that lead to irresponsibility and

[2] "Your Will," words and music by Darius Brooks from *Your Will* by Darius Brooks, © 2004, EMI Gospel.

failure just because you do not understand why you were hurt. Instead, cling to Him and accept that He can bring you through anything, and when you get to heaven, He will then give you the understanding—but you have to make it there first.

- A big part of learning to forget has to do with trusting God, knowing that He will use the bruised knees and sore tailbones to get you from point A to B and beyond. What others have meant for harm God can and does use to bring about good in our lives. (See Genesis 50:20.) When we recognize this, we will be more apt to let go of some of the smoldering coals of unforgiveness and start putting the painful, harmful episodes of our lives behind us.

- Coach yourself to first forgive—the feeling will come later. Then, lock it in so you cannot so easily go back and pick it up, by confessing to an accountability partner that you have done so.

- The Scriptures tell us, *"A merry heart does good, like medicine"* (Proverbs 17:22 NKJV). A big part of the healing process and learning to forget is remembering to smile and laugh again.

- Keep your hope alive, and remember that you will have better days!

- Guard against complete exhaustion happening frequently, or you are only asking for trouble in forgetting past injuries. I know it may sound simple, but taking time off and sometimes just getting a good night's sleep goes a long way during those times you are trying to put the past behind you. Go to bed! Then, when you get up, determine that you are going to do something fun to restore your joy.

- People who take themselves and life too seriously will ultimately find themselves having a hard time looking beyond the faults and offenses of others. Determine today that tomorrow will not be so serious. Let the fun begin, and you just might find the strength to forget the sting of pain in the midst of your joyfulness!

- Turn right and "let the jerk go." Continuing to chase down every person who offends you in life and attempting to make them pay will only exercise the muscle of unforgiveness and bitterness.

- The quicker you learn the fruit that suffering produces, the quicker you can move on!

- The past will release you if you find your purpose for the future. And you just might find that God has used even those past offenses to teach you priceless lessons that you could

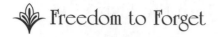

have learned no other way about how to proceed in that purpose!

• Stop confessing that you will never forget.
Release the person you have forgiven of the
guilt (or you have not really forgiven them),
and confess out loud (to yourself and the
devil) that you are releasing them. Then, let
the forgetting begin.

• If your only associates and friends are those
who are somber, sad, and validating your
despair, find yourself some new friends.
Laugh with some new faces!

• One definition of *forget* is "to fail to recall."
It is active. It denotes choice. Life has too
much to offer to let a day be wasted on bitterness. If children can refuse to fuss about
roadkill when they could be climbing lilac
trees and setting bear traps, then we can
fail to recall yesterday's offenses for the sake
of the important things we are facing in our
lives today.

• Set some goals. When goals become a focus,
you will find that hurts and pains move
down the priority list. Not only that, but
the achieving of them (another reason it is
important to set more realistic baby-step
goals) will do a lot to encourage us and give
us hope to move beyond the despair of yesterday's tragedies.

- Do not let pride keep you from admitting you were hurt, thereby burying a living bitterness in your psyche. Make up your mind that when you fail and people criticize, you will not stop taking risks just because you may fail. Any of these attitudes may cause a passive-aggressive bitterness to well up within.

- Connectivity with others can make all the difference in the world to someone in pain. Sometimes I have received nothing more than a warm smile given to me across a crowded room, and it made me feel like I was loved, respected, and appreciated. It enabled me to stand a little taller and move on.

- Plead now for the blood Jesus to be applied to the one who hurt you—that person who seems to be doing so well. Declare, "I will not go to a cold grave early because of bitterness or jealousy. Jealousy helps you remember offenses, not forget them. Declare, "I am free from jealousy and the need for vengeance in the name of Jesus Christ!"

- The quickest way become to unsettled again when face-to-face with the one who hurt you is to get rattled; so be classy but not aloof, humble but not arrogant, cordial but not shut-down. Then, as soon as you are away from them, genuinely bless them! Take a look at the pattern our Lord established on the cross: though He was rejected by all men—even those closest to him—yet He prayed for a blessing that they would be forgiven and not be held accountable. This is all an effective part of the follow-up therapy.

- Sometimes you need to get away. There is something so deep about realizing there are opportunities outside of your four walls. The sun does shine in other places. There is a whole lot more to the world if you are pushed to explore it. You will be able to come back from your break with a renewed strength and vigor to go on.

- If reconciliation can be accomplished (whether weeks, months, or years later), it goes a long way toward helping us forget the past and pressing forward.

- Having the right attitude of gratitude toward God for whatever comes your way "turns the light on," so that even what was meant to harm you has been used to advance and mature you.

- It is easier to let go of other's abrasiveness, rudeness, and cruelty when you realize God just used them to knock off some of the rough edges you had—rough edges that may have caused others debilitating damage or may have kept you out of a whole new level of intimacy with Him.

As you will see in the appendixes, there are two patterns of thought that can help you renew your mind and rid yourself of the pain.

The first is to make your own "fun things to remember" list. Post it on the refrigerator. In the process of forgetting, we often need to fill up the vacuum of what we want to forget with things we want to remember. It is fun to remember and goes a long way to helping us learn to forget.

The second is to pick up the Scriptures and read the many times God kept His people, gave them hope, supplied their needs, and gave them victories out of hardship. Then make a list of your favorite stories to remind yourself that if "God is for you, who can be against you?" (See Romans 8:31.) And if He did it for them, He will do it for you.

> Forget what is behind and press onward toward the higher places of God.

I once had a friend who, every time I said, "I didn't know that," would respond with, "Well, now you know, and knowing is half the battle." Hopefully the outcome of this book is that you have learned how to forget the painfulness and sorrow of past hurts. You may have forgiven but did not know what to do with the scar tissue. Any spiritual methods or truths can only be applied and effective as they are utilized in an intimate dependency on a living and loving God. *"If*

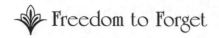

my people, which are called by my name, shall humble themselves, and pray...then will I hear...and heal their land" (2 Chronicles 7:14).

So, lean upon God, not on your own understanding; acknowledge Him in all your ways (see Proverbs 3:5); and regarding offenses do this one thing: forget what is behind and press onward toward the higher places He is calling you to.

Appendixes

Appendix 1

Fun Things to Remember

Remembering that there are a lot of good, humorous, and delightful moments in life will go a long way to helping us realize that the bad, ugly, and hurtful moments are only a part of the journey.

I would suggest you make your own list of delightful moments you have had in your life and place it somewhere you will often see it. It will remind you, even in some of the sadder, darker times, that life has many precious and amazing moments as well.

In the process of forgetting, we need to replace the things we want to forget with things we want to remember. It is healthy to remember the good, the precious, the encouraging moments in life, and they are very effective in helping us learn to forget.

Here are a few of my favorite things:

1. The wave of a stranger who thought you were someone else.
2. Your wave back to them.

3. A baby's cooing (with dribble as a side dish).

4. The perfume of an elderly lady.

5. A little boy laughing in the park.

6. Warm, snugly blankets on a cold night.

7. A good hair day.

8. The ten-dollar bill you found in your pocket from last week.

9. Food on the boss' chin.

10. That eerie, but beautiful color in the sky before a storm.

11. The first whiff you catch of hamburgers being grilled.

12. Your nose and mouth prints on a clean window.

13. Your spouse's singing in the shower.

14. Peanut butter on pancakes.

15. Your best friend's hugs.

16. An all-green-light trip to work.

17. Telling others how you "used to be skinny."

18. Ice cream cones you ate secretly.

19. Searching for your "lost" car in the mall parking lot.

20. Cinnamon cider at Christmas.

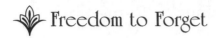 Freedom to Forget

Add your own favorite things to this list and turn to it when you need help remembering the good things in life.

My List of Fun Things to Remember

_____

_____

_____

_____

_____

_____

_____

_____

_____

_____

_____

_____

_____

_____

_____

_____

_____

_____

_____

_____

Appendix 1: Fun Things to Remember

My List of Fun Things to Remember

_____

_____

_____

_____

_____

_____

_____

_____

_____

_____

_____

_____

_____

_____

_____

_____

_____

_____

_____

_____

_____

_____

Appendix 2

Remembering Who God Is

D are I, as a preacher, say that one of the reasons we might not be so good at forgetting and getting beyond the pains of our past is because we may be lacking in knowledge of how God used the worst of circumstances in His people's lives in the Bible to show them the blessing and benefit of serving Him? Maybe if you are not familiar with one or more of the above, you should take the time to open your Bible and find some of these stories.

One of my favorite passages in the Bible is Psalm 119:165, *"Great peace have they which love thy law: and nothing shall offend them."* From this, I garner that the more we have hidden God's Word in our hearts and understand His providence and provision, the less likely we will even let people offend us. From practicing this passage, I have come to the conclusion that I am more in control of not getting offended than others are in offending me.

Appendix 2: Remembering Who God Is

Pick up the Scriptures. Read the many times God kept His people, gave them hope, supplied their needs, and gave them victories out of hardship. Then make a list of your favorite stories to remind yourself that "if God is for you, who can be against you?" (See Romans 8:31.) Here are the ones I especially like:

1. Noah's rainbow. (See Genesis 9:13–16.)

2. Abraham's ram. (See Genesis 22:13.)

3. Moses' dry ground. (See Exodus 14:16–22.)

4. Solomon's wisdom. (See 1 Kings 4:29.)

5. Elijah's raven. (See 1 Kings 17:2–6.)

6. Job's honor. (See Job 42:12–17.)

7. David's psalms of thanksgiving. (See Psalm 26:7; 95:2; 100:4; and 147:7 for example.)

8. Hannah's proof. (See 1 Samuel 1:1–20.)

9. Isaiah's hope. (See Isaiah 8:17.)

10. Jeremiah's fire. (See Jeremiah 43:12.)

11. Ezekiel's visions. (See Ezekiel 1.)

12. Shadrach, Meshach, and Abednego's firefighter. (See Daniel 3.)

13. Daniel's lion tamer. (See Daniel 6:11–24.)

14. Jonah's submarine. (See Jonah 1:17–2:10.)

15. Lazarus' chance to really "liven" things up. (See John 11:1–44.)

16. The prodigal's only hope for jewelry. (See Luke 15:11–24.)

17. Paul's lighting coordinator. (See Acts 9:1–18.)

18. Paul and Silas' "Jailhouse Rock" soundtrack. (See Acts 16:23–26.)

19. Jude's last chance to get published in a best-seller. (See Jude.)

20. Caterer to parties of 4,000 or more! (See Matthew 14:17–21; Mark 15:34–36, for example.)

And don't forget Ruth, Esther, Mary, Joseph, and others! You can write down your favorite Bible stories as a reference for inspiration when you need a reminder of who God is. If He can do these things for people in the past, He will certainly provide miracles for you!

My Reminders of Who God Is

_____

_____

_____

_____

_____

_____

_____

_____

_____

_____

Appendix 2: Remembering Who God Is

My Reminders of Who God Is

_____

_____

_____

_____

_____

_____

_____

_____

_____

_____

_____

_____

_____

_____

_____

_____

_____

_____

_____

_____

_____

_____

_____

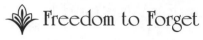 Freedom to Forget

My Reminders of Who God Is

_____

_____

_____

_____

_____

_____

_____

_____

_____

_____

_____

_____

_____

_____

_____

_____

_____

_____

_____

_____

Addenda

Addendum 1

Learning to Sing
the Hard Songs
(Especially Dedicated to Music Ministers)

*By the rivers of Babylon, there we sat down, yea,
we wept, when we remembered Zion. We hanged
our harps upon the willows in the midst thereof.
For there they that carried us away captive required
of us a song; and they that wasted us required of
us mirth, saying, Sing us one of the songs of Zion.
How shall we sing the Lord's song in a strange land?
If I forget thee, O Jerusalem, let my right hand
forget her cunning. If I do not remember thee, let
my tongue cleave to the roof of my mouth; if I
prefer not Jerusalem above my chief joy.*
—Psalm 137:1–6

An educated listener perceives and responds to
music with his total being—as tonal stimuli
relate to one another by the tastes and habits

of the human mind, which is filtered and processed by a selective auditory nervous system. Every facet of behavior—physiological and psychological, motor and mental—becomes attuned to, and congruent with, the structure of musical events. Through such empathetic identification, music is quite literally *felt*.

Humans responding to the ethos of music know that it may lead them to be sad or joyful, restrained or exuberant, calm or agitated. Cadence, sonority, tempo, dynamics, and register all play a crucial role in defining the character of a musical event.

In plain English (for all you non-musicians who are reading this), it is more than just sitting down at a keyboard and playing chords and repetitious rhythms. It is more than just standing up to a microphone and rendering a melody or pattern of words.

> When the hard times come in life, you must learn to sing the hard songs.

You are about to illuminate, delight, fascinate, encourage, implicate, and convey a spirit, an attitude or feeling. You will either move people to continuity and mobility with the Holy Spirit of God, or you will create degrees of inhibition and obstruction to the liberty of the Spirit and the congruency of worship. It will either be perfect harmony or frightening discord with the Spirit.

We may have intricate harmonies, proper tonguing, arpeggiated chromatic clusters, and a glissando in the proper place, but alas, it can still be *"as sounding brass or a tinkling cymbal"* (1 Corinthians 13:1). Music is, in her health and soundness, the teacher of perfect order, but in her depravity, she is also the teacher of perfect disorder and disobedience.

Your spirit set to a tune will either incite people to riot or revival. The quality is not all-important—your voice may sound like asthma set to music and still be a rhapsodic aria to God's glory.

One of the saddest accounts in the Bible is unfolded before us in Psalm 137. Israel, with all her beautiful singers, talented harpists, and choreographed worshippers, was taken captive into a heathen and pagan land—not through the fault of others, but through her own vacillating back and forth to sin and backsliding.

Their joy had departed, their enthusiastic music and expressive singing was silent, and finally they sat down by the rivers of Babylon, crying and watching the shifting currents from the riverbank. The only melodic sound they heard then was an occasional isolated note, as a bird fluttered past the strings of their sacred harps hung high in the willow trees. Their vibrato stilled and emotions drained, their fluency of rhythm had faded into a stark, deadened silence.

Then they remembered Jerusalem.

Then they remembered a new dance of sweet refreshings from their God.

Then they remembered choir practice and the joy of lifting their voices in corporate praise.

Then they remembered a sermon on a pure spirit toward their brother.

Then they remembered the importance of a faithful attitude.

But it was too late. They never learned how to sing the hard songs of life. Now they were forced to lift their gifted voices only for their entertainment value to the enemy.

All I have to give is what He has given me to share.

_____

They were singing the Lord's song in a strange land.

Their lament should become the watchword for every musician, soloist, choir director, and singer:

> *If I forget thee, O Jerusalem, let my right hand forget her cunning. If I do not remember thee, let my tongue cleave to the roof of my mouth; if I prefer not Jerusalem above my chief joy.*
>
> (Psalm 137:5–6)

Not my keyboard, not my solo, not "Did you enjoy our musical renditions and my vocal gymnastics?", but "Did you enjoy Jesus?" All I have to give is what He has given me to share.

If you do not learn to sing the hard songs of life, you will wind up beside the rivers of Babylon. You will be singing the Lord's song in a strange land, doing what you never dreamed you would do.

I have heard some say, "I cannot live for God; there are too many hypocrites. I cannot sing that hard song." If those hypocrites can come between you and God, then they are closer to God than you are.

Sing on. Sing the hard songs.

"Life has not treated me fairly." Expecting life to treat you fairly because you are a good person is as ludicrous as expecting a bull not to ram you because you are a vegetarian.

Sing on. Sing the hard songs.

When you have done all you can, yet you are mis-understood, sing on.

When you have given and not received, loved with-out reciprocation, sacrificed only to be slain, sing on. Sing the hard songs.

If they forgot to mention your name, remember Johann Wenzel Tomaschek and Hugo Vorisek. They were two of the greatest composers who ever penned melodies; they authored more compositions than Bach and Beethoven combined. Today, their melodies are unheard and their names unrecognized, yet they have contributed volumes of musical brilliance to the archives of orchestrated symphonies.

Addendum 1: Learning to Sing the Hard Songs

Sing on! If someone else gets the credit you deserved, sing the hard songs. It takes work to leave a melody people will remember when you have gone on to your eternal reward.

Sing on. Sing the hard songs.

Easy songs are those times when living for God has thrust you into the limelight and you are singing the solo—you are the star, the one performing to fanfare.

The hard songs are those times when all your efforts seem to no avail, when others receive accolades instead of you, when it is hard to pay your tithes and then your bills, and when it is hard to love those whom you perceive as "getting all the breaks."

Sing on. Sing the hard songs.

The hard songs sometimes slow down when you want to speed ahead, walk when you want to run, plateau when you want to coast, but sing the hard songs anyway. Soon the Conductor will give the signal to the musicians on the keyboards and the choir members in the chorus of life, and—with one triumphant crescendo—He will raise His Director's baton, and

We shall not all sleep, but we shall all be changed, in a moment, in the twinkling of an eye, at the last trump: for the trumpet shall sound, and the dead shall be raised incorruptible, and we shall be changed.

(1 Corinthians 15:51–52)

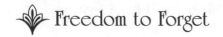 Freedom to Forget

Do not get too wrapped up in your own lyrics, your own composition, and your own cadence. Watch the Conductor for our song is in the last refrain.

Gospel singer Sallie Martin learned to sing the hard songs. As she lay dying in excruciating pain, her life a gallery of inspiration, she wrote,

I want to dig a little deeper,
Dig a little deeper in the storehouse of His love.

Sing on when the pain wracks your mind, body and heart. Sing the hard songs.

Thomas Dorsey, weak after standing at the casket of his wife and child (who had both died suddenly in 1932), composed his masterpiece:

Precious Lord, take my hand.
Lead me on, let me stand.
I am tired, I am weak, I am worn.
Through the storm, through the night
Lead me on to the light.
Take my hand, precious Lord,
Lead me home.

When my way grows drear,
Precious Lord, linger near.
When my life is almost gone,
At the river, Lord I'll stand.
Guide my feet, hold my hand.
Take my hand, precious Lord,
Lead me home.

Addendum 1: Learning to Sing the Hard Songs

If Charles Wesley is a Cadillac and Thomas Dorsey is a Rolls Royce, and I am just an old Model T—but I can drive without shifting gears or hitting reverse and make it over the hill—that is what counts, my friend!

I am going to learn to sing the hard songs.

Sing on. Sing the hard songs, and, in doing so, you will forget the pain.

Isn't there a way to start over again?
Isn't there a way to be happy within?
What would it take sorrows past to erase?
I wonder...is there a way?

I traveled many years down life's hard road.
I was burdened with such a heavy load.
Then somebody told me about nail-scarred hands.
They were reaching down to pick up a fallen man.
Shackles fell off and I became free.
I could hardly believe He would do it for me.

Jesus is the way to start over again.
He's the only way to be happy within.
There is no heartache or load He won't bear.
Just give Him your life today.

"Isn't There a Way?" words and music Rev. Dan Willis from *Live in Kingston Jamaica—We All Need Somebody!* By Rev. Dan Willis & the Pentecostals of Chicago, ©1997, Tyscot, Inc.

Addendum 2

How to Forget
(For Those in Spiritual Leadership)

Most of us have a tendency or desire to "walk away" from responsibility when we are emotionally drained. Ever felt like running? People who run get tired quickly, never have anything to show for all their running, and are not respected by very many people unless they are running in such a way to win the race. The Bible says, *"He that endureth to the end shall be saved"* (Matthew 10:22).

If you as a leader spend your whole life trying to run from people who have hurt you, you will never amount to anything. I know Christians who have a calling from God on their lives, but they cannot take criticism and "let it go." They can sing, preach, and perform, but when faced with criticism, they attack and either send the sheep running or they run themselves (and sometimes both).

I have observed people who have pastored churches for a long time. I have observed politicians who were reelected for three or four terms of office. I have observed businessmen who maintained thriving businesses for thirty to forty years. They all had one thing in common—they were committed to their causes!

In spite of being talked about...

In spite of being lied about...

In spite of having frustrations...

In spite of a lack of finances...

In spite of severe injustices...

They remained committed!

If it was time to go to work, they worked.

If it was time to preach, they preached.

If it was time to stand, they stood.

If it was time to give, they gave.

Commitment means a pledge or promise to do something.

They were bound by a promise.

I think that is where we are lacking sometimes. We run away rather than stick it out. But as I have traveled the globe, I have also watched people who run. They keep on running—and even though the names change, people are the same everywhere. They don't realize they are facing the same devil that made them run from the last place they were. It is amazing how I have observed the same people with the same characteristics in every church.

Years ago, I prayed for God to move a lady out of my ministry—one of the few times I have ever taken that drastic an approach. I prayed this so long and so fervently that God finally did as I asked—and then promptly sent me two who were in worse shape in her place. I found myself pleading for God to send me back my first troublemaker! And I never asked God to move anyone again.

Instead, I learned a little key to survival from a dear friend. Many criticized me for attempting to pastor a church in Chicago at sixteen years of age; they said I wouldn't last six months. Many of them are gone now, and I am still standing. And here is that survival tip passed on to me by my friend: "If you act the way you want to feel long enough, pretty soon you will feel the way you are acting." I cannot tell you how many times that was all I had to go on!

> As I sang, I got happy. As I danced, I got joy. As I loved, I felt love.

When it was time to sing, I sang with every fiber of my being.

I preached on those nights, not because I felt like it, but because it was my commitment. I learned it was therapeutic for me.

As I sang, I got happy.

As I preached, I got free.

As I danced, I got joy.

As I loved, I felt love.

In pain? A victim of unfair and brutal scrutiny? Feeling alone? Tired of the spotlight? Do not run!

Stand still! Regroup. Then, march on.

Sing anyway; preach anyhow; love them anyhow. When you do not know what the right thing is to do, follow through with your commitments.

My motto for leaders who must work under pressure or when they feel like running is: "Heads up, shoulders back, put your smile on, and march." The devil has nothing on you because you are covered with the blood of Jesus. Your joy will return, the victory will come, and your bad memories of it all will fade when you get in the presence of the great Mind Fixer!

Do not make excuses for not following through with your commitments, and when you need encouragement, consider Calvary.

About the Author

About the Author

Dan Willis did not exactly envision a life in ministry as a young boy growing up in Chicago. Though he loved the contagious rhythms of gospel music, he never knew he'd one day be creating them himself. Yet from these humble beginnings developed one of today's leading pastors and gospel artists.

As a young boy, Dan's dreams actually involved entering the medical field as a neurosurgeon until the fateful day when, at age sixteen, he was called to "temporarily" take over the pastor position of a local church that had lost theirs. Thirty years later, Dan is still there, serving as the senior pastor of The Lighthouse Church of All Nations in Alsip, Illinois. Never wavering, he took the small ministry of sixteen people and nurtured it into a thriving multi-cultural body of over 1,500, which is now preparing to build a new, state-of-the-art sanctuary and community center.

The driving force of Dan's ministry has always been one of uniting the races. To look out over the crowd on a typical Sunday morning you will see men, women, and children from over fifty different nationalities as the last census revealed. Each Sunday is spent celebrating one of the unique cultures, and he implements a plethora of innovative ways to bring acceptance and understanding through the love of Christ.

Confronting the walls of racism and prejudice is never easy, but music has been a tool Dan has used to share his message. Dan is a gifted singer, musician, and producer. In 1990 he founded a community choir called The Pentecostals of Chicago. It was a groundbreaking move at the time because it brought together black, white, Hispanic, and Asian singers from over twenty Chicago area churches. This group, now known as The All Nations Choir, has six albums to its credit and has performed with artists from Celine Dion to Kirk Franklin and on missionary trips to the orphanages of Kingston, Jamaica.

Most recently you can also add "executive producer" to Dan's journey as the creator and host of *Inspiration Sensation,* a televised Christian music talent search. Seeing the need for young men and women to have a faith-filled outlet for their talents, he is now in the fourth season of this Emmy-Award-winning program. Dan has traveled the country ministering and teaching to men and women through the Starting Line Prison Fellowship organization and has

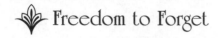

also been a national and international speaker on the topics of music, ministry, racial reconciliation, leadership, and community development.

What does the future hold for this extraordinary man of God? Only time will tell. Though he did not become the physician he once dreamed of becoming, he is still touching and healing lives through his powerful gifts and generous heart.

You may contact the author at:
The Lighthouse Church of All Nations
Chicago's "Bridging the Gap" Church
4501 W. 127th Street
Alsip, IL 60803
(708) 385-6020
www.thelighthousechurch.org

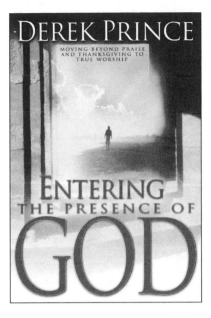

Entering the Presence of God:
Moving Beyond Praise and Thanksgiving to True Worship
Derek Prince

"The harder I try to be good, the worse off I am!" If that sounds like you, there's good news. Internationally acclaimed Bible teacher Derek Prince shows the way to victorious intimacy with God as he explains how you can enter into His very presence to embrace the spiritual, physical, and emotional blessings of true worship. Learn the secrets of entering into His rest, fellowshipping with the Lord, receiving divine revelation from God's Spirit, and conducting spiritual warfare. Discover how to be freed from the bondage of guilt and sin and obtain an inner peace and joy that nothing else can duplicate. Don't miss out on the thrill of worship…God's way!

ISBN: 978-0-88368-719-2 • Trade • 176 pages

www.whitakerhouse.com

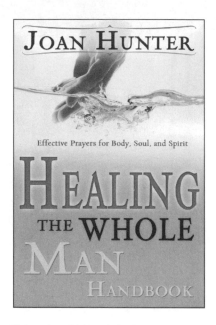

Healing the Whole Man Handbook:
Effective Prayers for Body, Soul, and Spirit
Joan Hunter

You can walk in divine health and healing. The secrets to God's words for healing and recovery are in this comprehensive, easy-to-follow guidebook containing powerful healing prayers that cover everything from abuse to yeast infections and everything in between.

Truly anointed with the gifts of healing, Joan Hunter has over thirty years of experience praying for the sick and brokenhearted and seeing them healed and set free. By following these step-by-step instructions and claiming God's promises, you can be healed, set free, and made totally whole—body, soul, and spirit!

ISBN: 978-0-88368-815-8 • Trade • 240 pages

WHITAKER
HOUSE

www.whitakerhouse.com

Free at Last:
Removing the Past from Your Future
(with Study Guide CD)
Larry Huch

You can break free from your past! Don't let what has happened
to you and your family hold you back in life. You can find freedom
from depression, anger, abuse, insecurity, and addiction in Jesus
Christ. Pastor Larry Huch reveals powerful truths from Scripture
that enabled him and many others to quickly break the destructive
chains in their lives and receive God's blessings. Learn the secret
to true freedom and you, too, can regain your joy and hope,
experience divine health, mend broken relationships,
walk in true prosperity—body, soul, and spirit.

ISBN: 978-0-88368-428-3 • Trade with CD • 272 pages

WHITAKER
HOUSE

www.whitakerhouse.com

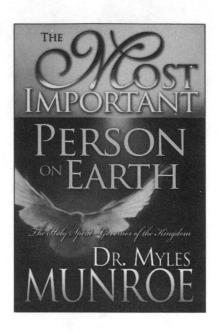

The Most Important Person on Earth:
The Holy Spirit, Governor of the Kingdom

Dr. Myles Munroe

In *The Most Important Person on Earth*, Dr. Myles Munroe explains
how the Holy Spirit is the Governor of God's kingdom on earth,
much as royal governors administered the will of earthly kings
in their territories. Under the guidance and enabling of the Holy
Spirit, you will discover how to bring order to the chaos in your life,
receive God's power to heal and deliver, fulfill your true purpose
with joy, become a leader in your sphere of influence, and be part of
God's government on earth. Enter into the fullness of God's Spirit
as you embrace God's design for your life today.

ISBN: 978-0-88368-986-8 • Hardcover • 320 pages

www.whitakerhouse.com